Where
Is God?

Where Is God?

A Personal Story of

Finding God

in Grief and Suffering

JOHN S. FEINBERG

BROADMAN
&HOLMAN
PUBLISHERS

NASHVILLE, TENNESSEE

0–8054–3041–5

Published by Broadman & Holman Publishers
Nashville, Tennessee

Dewey Decimal Classification: 362.2
Subject Heading: HUNTINGTON'S
DISEASE—CARE \ BRAIN—DISEASES

1 2 3 4 5 6 7 8 9 10 10 09 08 07 06 05 04

Dedicated to

Josiah Stephen
Jonathan Seth
Jeremy Samuel

Three gifts of God's love

CONTENTS

PREFACE

There are many hurting people in our world today. No one knows when and where tragedy may occur. Sometimes because we haven't faced serious affliction, we think it won't happen to us. Especially if we live our lives in conformity to God's Word, we assume that we won't have to face certain horrible kinds of tragedies. Christians know the story of Job, but everyone agrees that his was a special case. It is assumed that most who suffer so terribly do so in punishment for some serious sin.

All of these common conceptions seemed worthless when my family learned something far beyond our worst fears. This book recounts what happened and what I have learned as a result. This is not a book that I ever would have dreamed of writing. Even more, I wish I hadn't learned the things I shall share in the way I did. But God's will and way for us don't always match what we would like to happen. Hence, I have a story to tell that I never would have imagined. I share it because I hope it will help you if you are suffering, and because I trust that it will help others to minister to the afflicted.

An earlier version of this book has been in print before, but eventually it became time for a reprint. The publisher asked that I expand it somewhat and that I bring readers up to date on what has happened to my family since I last wrote about this. I have done so. The major themes of the earlier edition have not changed, but I have amplified many of them. In addition, over the years I have come to see new things that I present now in this edition.

Since this book is about personal struggles with suffering and evil, some may wonder why I have made no reference to other classical treatments of the topic. C. S. Lewis's classic *A Grief Observed*, D. A. Carson's *How Long, Oh Lord?* and Nicholas Wolterstorff's *Lament for a Son* are all very well worth reading. I have not referred to them only because this book is the story of my family, and what has happened is in various ways unique. The story is a very personal one, one that I would just as soon have kept private. However, through the leading of the Lord and the encouragement of others, I have seen that I should write about our story, but I wanted this to be *our* story told in *my* own way and words. It isn't a research project, but rather a personal testimony of God's specific dealings with me and my family.

To produce any book requires the encouragement and help of other people. I must initially express my appreciation to Leonard Goss and Broadman & Holman Publishers. Their willingness to reprint this work, along with their suggestions about changes that could be made, have been most helpful. In addition, I want to thank the administration and board of Trinity Evangelical Divinity School for granting a sabbatical leave during which I reworked this book. And then, I have greatly benefited from the love and support of my wife and family. In addition, I believe you will find Pat's "Afterword" (which she hasn't revised from the earlier edition) to be moving and encouraging as you confront your own trials and afflictions.

If you are confronting suffering at this time, I hope that this book will minister to you. Some things in the book may bear rereading at a later time when you have had more time to deal with the problems that you confront. The things that have been and are helpful to me didn't happen all at the same time, so I fully understand that you may find parts of this book helpful at one time and others helpful at another. I also hope that this book will be of value to those who minister to the afflicted. May God be pleased to use it in these ways to his glory!

CHAPTER 1

PRELUDE TO A PROBLEM

Many Christians love to sing the hymns "Have Thine Own Way, Lord" and "Where He Leads Me I Will Follow." These hymns express a basic longing of every Christian, the desire to know and obey God's will. But is it possible to know God's will for our lives?

Will God reveal his will, if we seek it? Does he ever hide information from us in order to get us to do his will? Is it possible to seek God's will, find it and do it, and then discover that what God wanted brought great suffering and evil into your life? If that happened wouldn't it mean that God had tricked or even deceived you into doing his will?

Preposterous, you reply! That couldn't happen. Such questions aren't even worth considering, for God just doesn't work that way. Scripture tells us to seek God's will and to pray for it. Jesus told his disciples that when they pray, they should ask God to do his will on earth as it is done in heaven (Matt. 6:10). So, of course, God's people should ask him to do his will in their own lives. In fact, the apostle John offers the following encouragement: "And this is the confidence which we have before Him, that, if we ask anything according to His will, He hears us. And if we know that He hears us in whatever we ask, we know that we have the requests which we have asked from Him" (1 John 5:14–15 NASB).

There you have it. We must seek God's will and as long as we pray in accordance with it, he will grant our requests. But if we pray according to God's will, he wouldn't give us something evil, would he? After all, remember what Jesus said: "Or what man is there among you, when his son shall ask him for a loaf, will give him a stone? Or if he shall ask for a fish, he will not give him a snake, will he? If you then, being evil, know how to give good gifts to your children, how much more shall your Father who is in heaven give what is good to those who ask Him!" (Matt. 7:9–11 NASB).

Surely, then, if God reveals his will and we do it, evil won't befall us. God won't give us a stone when we ask for a loaf or a snake when we ask for a fish, especially not when we ask according to his will for us. Thoughts to the contrary must be absurd, if not blasphemous. They imagine the unthinkable, the impossible.

Or do they? For most of my life I would not have even thought to raise such questions. Oh, I knew bad things happen to good people, and for much of my life I had wondered why God lets this happen if he really loves us. As I grew up I was fascinated by the story of Job, especially with what we learn in Job 1–2 about how it all began. Being Jewish by background I heard my parents speak frequently about the Holocaust, and I was horrified at such inhumanity to man. Even more, I couldn't understand how a loving God would allow this to happen to his "chosen people." And then, there was my mother. I can't remember a time while growing up when she wasn't ill or in the hospital with some physical problem or another. She was seldom so ill for days on end that she couldn't do her duties in the home. But I could tell that she constantly did her work while having to deal with a great deal of pain.

That's not the whole story about my mother, however. Her life had been filled with persecution. She was born in a little Ukrainian village in the early twentieth century. Peasants at that time didn't matter to the government, and Jewish peasants were worth even less. Not long after her birth, the Bolshevik Revolution came to Russia. In the midst of the persecution, she and her family fled from their homeland and came to America. But the experiences of cruelty at the hands of soldiers and hiding to avoid capture left indelible marks on her personality. For many years after she and my father married, she would still have nightmares about her childhood.

All of this made me ask why a God of love would allow such things to happen to innocent people. At various times in my life I thought about such things and pondered whether I would still want to worship and serve God if he rewarded my faithfulness with severe affliction. But I didn't expect to address such questions, because I never dreamed that terrible affliction might come in the process of seeking, finding, and doing God's will. Nor would I have thought that God's ways might include getting someone to do his will by withholding information—information which, if known, would have kept them from doing what God wanted, but also would have avoided much personal pain and anguish. That would seem like trickery, even deceit, and it would also be cruel, especially if by doing God's will we wound up in the midst of severe affliction. Who would think God does this to get his way?

And yet, in the late 1980s something happened that led me to raise these questions and to think the unthinkable. For reasons mentioned above, throughout my life I have thought a lot about the problem of evil, the question of why there is evil and suffering in our world if there is a God who loves us enough to stop it and has enough power to do so. In fact, I even wrote my doctoral dissertation in philosophy on the problem of evil. I had learned that there is a difference between asking why there is evil *in general* if an all-loving, all-powerful God exists, and asking why God allows a *specific* evil to happen to someone.

Philosophers and theologians debate on the intellectual level how the evil in our world is consistent with an all-powerful, all-loving God. On the other hand, the *personal experience of* evil creates a different kind of problem. Those dealing with personal affliction may find that their suffering disrupts their relation to God. They may find it hard to serve or even worship God. They may even be tempted to stop believing in God altogether. The personal experience of evil precipitates a crisis of faith in the believer's life. As one philosopher wisely observes, "Such a problem calls, not for philosophical enlightenment, but for pastoral care."[1]

I read that statement many years ago. Intellectually, I agreed with it, but experientially, I didn't really understand it. I had always seen the problem of evil as a major hindrance to getting non-Christians to consider Christ. I knew it could be devastating to the faith of Christians as well. But I thought that as long as one had intellectual answers to explain why God allowed evil in the world, that would satisfy those who suffer. The intellectual answers would give the necessary strength to withstand the afflictions. Even more, I thought that if comforters could just point to all the positive things God might do in the lives of sufferers in the midst of their trials, the afflicted might reach a point where they could even thank God for the affliction.

When I saw others struggle in their relationship with God because of some tragedy, I naively thought that if I could just talk with them and offer some intellectual answers, that would resolve everything. I was somewhat impatient with them when they seemed unable to move past these struggles. In principle, I agreed that sufferers need pastoral care, but I thought that a lot of that care involved explaining intellectually God's purposes in allowing evil. Maybe personal struggles in the face of evil aren't problems needing philosophical enlightenment, but a healthy dose of academic philosophy couldn't hurt. Or so I thought.

Over the last decade and a half I have come to see things quite differently, especially because of the way evil has deeply touched my wife and family. Before these things happened, I couldn't have written this book. I thought it was enough just to have intellectual answers, and that those answers would be sufficient for handling any personal evil that might come into my life. For a long time after we learned about my wife's condition, I found it too painful to speak about what had happened, let alone write about it.

What happened that so revolutionized my thinking? Let me tell you my story. Like many people, I grew up, went to school, got married, and began a career in relatively trouble-free circumstances. There were problems and afflictions along the way, like most people experience, but nothing catastrophic or truly tragic. I knew that those who stand for Christ can expect to suffer, and I had a vivid illustration of that in my mother's constant faith despite illness after illness. I remembered as well that in the early 1950s my father had almost died, but God miraculously preserved his life. Dad had undergone an operation at the University of California, Los Angeles Medical Center, and recovery at home was going quite smoothly. But one evening after I had gone to bed he began to hemorrhage. No matter what Mom tried, the flow of blood continued. She called several local hospitals but was advised she had to take him to see his doctor. Unfortunately, the UCLA Med Center and Dad's doctor were some thirty-five to forty miles away. And this was in the days before the elaborate freeway system in Los Angeles had been built. The situation seemed hopeless, but Mom wouldn't give up. She got Dad and my sister (who was awake and helping by this time) in the car and set out for UCLA. By the time they arrived Dad had lost a substantial amount of blood. The doctors said his blood level was so low that he should have been dead. But he wasn't, and thankfully they were able to stabilize his condition. Dad recovered, but my realization that I could have lost my father showed me indelibly how tenuous a hold on life any of us has.

Because of these experiences, I figured that there were more troubles coming. I assumed that they would be like the rest I had endured—annoying, frustrating, and painful to a certain degree, but nothing totally devastating. After all, I reasoned, once one goes a certain distance with Christ and reaches a certain level of spiritual maturity, even really big problems won't derail spiritual growth. There might be temporary setbacks in one's relation to the Lord, but they would soon be over. Surely, Dad's near brush with death and Mom's continued faith, in spite of constantly dealing with painful physical problems, confirmed such thoughts.

All of that changed for me on November 4, 1987, when I learned something that went far beyond my worst nightmare. For some years my wife Pat had experienced certain physical difficulties. As best we can figure, she began to show signs of this disease as early as 1979. It manifested itself first as a periodic twitching of her shoulder. And, as each day wore on, Pat became extremely tired. These symptoms weren't painful, and neither Pat nor I thought of them as real physical problems. She thought that moving the shoulder was a habit that she could easily break. I thought her lack of energy wasn't unusual for a woman with two children under the age of five.

What we saw and how she felt were symptoms of something, but we had no idea of what. As the years passed, the difficulties became more pronounced. I had thought that the movements, now in other parts of her body as well, came about once every few minutes. One evening, however, without telling Pat, I decided to time how frequently she moved. To my surprise and dismay she had these movements every few seconds. This could no longer be interpreted as a habit that she could break. We decided that we had to find out what the problem was and get it corrected. She eventually went to a neurologist who made the diagnosis. When Pat came home from the doctor's office, I could tell something was wrong, but I never could have imagined what she was about to tell me. The doctor had diagnosed her as having Huntington's Chorea.

At that time, I didn't know what Huntington's Disease is. It is a genetically transmitted disease that involves the premature deterioration of brain cells deep within the brain. Brain cells are killed, and the result isn't entirely unlike what happens when an older person shows signs of dementia. With Huntington's Disease, symptoms are both physical and psychological. On the physical side, there is gradual loss of control of all voluntary bodily movement. In addition, Pat has problems keeping her balance and finds it harder and harder to walk more than a short distance. This physical deterioration has also slurred her speech and made it so hard to swallow that she must use a feeding tube. Her hand-eye coordination is sufficiently depleted that it is hard for her to use eating utensils, button a blouse, or zip up a jacket.

Huntington's also has mental and psychological effects. She initially began to forget things. That became worse, and gradually she has lost her ability to pay attention to anything for very long. All of this makes it increasingly difficult to follow the plot of a movie or television program, and reading a book is now basically a lost cause. Then, as with many Huntington's patients, depression is a major problem, though Pat takes medication for it and has responded well to that medication. Huntington's patients can also have hallucinations and ultimately become paranoid schizophrenic. Thankfully, so far we have seen neither of these last two symptoms, but one of the frustrating things about this disease is that you never know how rapidly it will progress or which symptoms anyone with it will exhibit. In fact, it is impossible to make any generalizations about the exact course of the disease, even if one uses the patient's own condition as the basis for predicting future symptoms. Some symptoms may never show themselves, while others that seemed initially transitory may never go away.

Though it is possible to begin to deal with Huntington's in one's teen years, symptoms usually begin when one is in her thirties or even her forties. It is a slow-developing disease, but over several decades it takes its toll, and it is fatal. Medications can minimize without removing symptoms completely, but there is no known cure. Only a few years before my wife's diagnosis had doctors even discovered the chromosome involved. It wasn't until 1993 that the exact genetic marker was discovered.

Though all of this is very bad news, the situation is even worse. Huntington's Disease is controlled by a dominant gene.

This means that only one parent needs to have it in order to transfer it to their children. Each child has a fifty-fifty chance of getting it, but symptoms don't usually start before one's thirties. Our three sons were born before Pat was diagnosed with the disease.

Since Huntington's is controlled by a dominant gene, those who have the gene get the disease. If they don't get the disease, they can't be a carrier. There are tests to determine beforehand how likely it is that one will have it. The accuracy of those tests increased as researchers zeroed in on and finally discovered the exact gene involved.

This raises an important question: Should children of a Huntington's carrier take the test or remain in the dark? I asked Pat's doctor what is involved in getting tested so that I could find out what percentage of the cost the health insurance company would cover. The doctor replied that whatever we did, we should avoid reporting any of it to the insurance company. If the test showed that one of our sons would get the disease, it might be impossible for him to get health insurance. It is also possible that an employer would refuse to hire someone known to have the gene for Huntington's. On the other hand, if our children don't know if they will get the disease, they must make decisions in the dark about career, marriage, and having children.

When this news came, my initial reaction was shock, confusion, and disbelief. How could this be happening? Before we were married, we knew that Pat's mother had mental problems. At the time of our wedding, she had been in a mental institution for five years. We asked several people how likely it was that this might happen to Pat, believing all along that it was a purely psychological problem. Psychologists assured us that if Pat were to have such problems, they would have already surfaced. Since she was in her twenties and nothing of that sort had happened, we were led to believe there was no need to worry. We never imagined that there was a physiological base to my mother-in-law's problems or that the difficulty could be passed genetically to my wife. Nor did anyone else. Immediate family members knew nothing about this, and others who might have known said nothing. My father-in-law had at one time heard the name of the disease, but didn't ask for details about it. Everyone who might have known the truth either didn't know it or withheld the information. Before we started our family, we checked again to see if anything hereditary could be passed on to harm the children. Again, we were reassured there was nothing to fear.

We had wanted to discover whether it was God's will for us to marry and later to have children. We had told God that we were willing to do whatever he wanted. If he didn't want us to marry, we asked that he show us that. One way to do so would be for us to learn that Pat would likely get her mother's disease. We searched for this information, but we didn't find it. When we didn't find such information, in addition to other factors I'll mention later, we were led to believe that God wanted us to marry.

In our thinking, none of this could possibly be happening, but it was. Professionals who were supposed to know about such things had said it wouldn't. I found it all very hard to believe. It was also unbelievable because of the basis of the doctor's diagnosis. He did nothing more than watch Pat move and ask her about her family history. No genetic tests or tests of any other kind were done that day, but the diagnosis was given. I complained that this was all too inferential. Such skimpy data shouldn't warrant that conclusion. No philosopher would accept that kind of argument. For several months I was torn between the hope that it wasn't true and fear that Pat's problems could be nothing else. When a second opinion by a specialist doing research on the disease confirmed the diagnosis, all hope that she didn't have Huntington's collapsed.

CHAPTER 2

HOW DISMAL
LIFE CAN SEEM

After my wife's initial diagnosis, I was besieged by a host of emotions and reactions. Even to this day, I still wrestle at times with some of those feelings. I believe others who experience tragedy undergo similar reactions. If we are to minister to those who are hurting, we must understand how they feel.

In chapter 1 I alluded to one of my initial reactions—denial. When Pat first told me the diagnosis, I asked on what basis the doctor made this assessment. Pat answered that he watched her move and asked about her family history. I asked if he did any tests and thought any should be done. There were no tests and no plans for any tests. I thought it was, therefore, absurd to offer such a horrible diagnosis on such flimsy evidence. Of course, at that time I knew nothing other than what Pat told me about Huntington's. Most other diseases I could think of had to be confirmed by some test or set of tests, so I thought the same must be true for this disease. Since Huntington's is caused by a defective gene, I couldn't believe that there was any certainty that Pat had it without doing a genetic test. To this day she has never had such a test, so certainly at the beginning I thought it impossible to find this diagnosis believable, based as it was on so little evidence.

I thought that it was good that I am a philosopher, because as one, I could detect faulty reasoning, and this was, I thought, a clear example of an inference unwarranted by the evidence.

But no amount of logic, philosophy, or any other sort of reasoning *proved* that the doctor was wrong! And so I had two reactions at once: belief that the doctor didn't know what he was talking about and fear that he was right after all! In the days and weeks that followed that first diagnosis, I did everything I could think of to disprove this "theory" about what was happening to Pat. Whenever I heard someone mention a disease, I asked about the symptoms, and if they seemed even vaguely like what Pat was experiencing, I imagined that her real problem was this other disease. But, whenever I asked a physician whether she might really have this "other" disease, the physician always had an explanation of why that couldn't be so. As we sought opinions from other doctors, I became more discouraged as they refuted theory after theory, but I felt this diagnosis had to be wrong because it had so little and such questionable (in my judgment) evidence to support it.

As we came closer to a "final" confirmation of the original diagnosis, I was still holding out hope that it wasn't so, but began to process what it would mean if the doctors were right. I can totally affirm that such an emotional state is no fun whatsoever. You are emotionally pulled in one direction by the defiant denial that this isn't really what's happening, and at the same time you are dragged in a conflicting direction by the realization of all the horrible implications, if the doctors were right. Torn between defiance and despair, one feels as if one has just endured a boxing match with the heavyweight champion of the world who has relentlessly pummeled your head and body round after round.

Denial at the outset isn't unusual when tragedy strikes. In my case, it lasted several months but came to a crushing end when we saw a doctor who was doing research on Huntington's. I brought him Pat's mother's chart, which the hospital in New York (where she spent the last decade of her life) sent upon my request; he observed Pat's symptoms, and confirmed that she had Huntington's. I raised one of my alternate theories, and he turned to the pages of the chart, pointed to several things and said emphatically, "That's Huntington's!" He also ordered a brain scan to confirm the diagnosis. The scan showed little deterioration at that point, but the fact that it showed any was evidence enough. By that point, however, I had already given up the fight—there simply were no adequate grounds to deny what had become painfully clear to all of us.

While I was hanging on to hope that the doctors were wrong but fearing the worst, and after confirmation that the diagnosis was correct, the predominant reactions I experienced were feelings of hopelessness and helplessness. There had been problems before, but usually there was some way out. In fact, I could usually figure out something to do. But, not this time. Huntington's is a disease with no known cure.

I felt that the situation was absolutely hopeless. I would have to watch my wife, whom I dearly love, slowly deteriorate and die. As the disease progressed, maybe she wouldn't even know me. Even worse, maybe she would know me, but would turn against me as she imagined that I had turned against her. After all, my mother-in-law had misjudged my father-in-law's reasons for putting her in a mental institution for the last years of her life. Irrational fears and feelings are the norm, not the exception with this disease. Eventually Pat would be gone, and yet it still wouldn't be over. The same thing could happen to each of our children. I remember thinking that this threat of doom would hang over me and my family every day for the rest of our lives. There was no morally acceptable way to escape this situation. There was only one person who could do anything about this, and it appeared at that time that God wasn't going to help. Beyond this, it seemed that he had led us into this situation rather than keeping us from it. As I reflected on the hopelessness of our situation, I realized how dismal life can seem.

Beyond the hopelessness, I felt helpless to do anything. I was experiencing physical problems myself that were only aggravated by the stress from this news. Before long I came to a point where I was barely able to do my work. I wasn't much help to my family either. I wanted at least to comfort Pat and help her deal with this distressing news, but all along she has handled this situation far better than I. Somehow God gave her strength and victory over the situation, and she didn't seem to need my help. I felt locked out of her life at this most critical time, as though I could be of little help. Whatever therapeutic value there might be for me in comforting her was lost.

The situation with the children wasn't much different. Before we told them what was happening, they knew something was wrong. I told Pat that we shouldn't trouble them with this news until we knew for certain that the diagnosis was correct. Once it was confirmed, we sat down with them and shared the news. Among other things, I told them that other people would probably say things about this disease that were wrong. Instead of listening to others, they should come and talk with us about it. If they had questions we couldn't answer, we would get the answers for them. Each understood some of what was happening, but all understood that their Mom was very sick. Over the years they have been hesitant to talk about the disease. When we would ask them how they were doing, they would say that they were doing fine and that they really didn't think about this disease much at all. Again, I was unable to offer them comfort as they seemed not to be bothered by what might happen to them. It has only been in recent years that they have been willing to share their feelings, and indeed they are very saddened by what is happening to their mother, and the chance that they could get this disease definitely colors their outlook on the future. But when we first broke the news to them (and for a long time after that), they didn't seem to need or want my comfort and encouragement about their situation.

Though the trials that confront you are probably different from mine, I suspect you have had similar feelings of hopelessness and helplessness if you have had to deal with some major tragedy. Along with those feelings comes a sense of abandonment. At such times, one feels that there is no answer and no help. Yes, there are friends and family, but what can they do? They aren't miracle-workers. Even the doctors can't cure this disease, so what could others do? Anyway, they have their own families to care for and their own problems to be concerned with.

Something else heightens the feeling of abandonment. Invariably when news like this comes, people are very concerned, but for various reasons, they tend to stay away. For example, they may be afraid that they will say the wrong thing and only make matters worse. Nobody wants to be like Job's comforters, so some people just stay away rather than taking the chance of sticking their foot in their mouth. Others may think that unless they have something "brilliant" to say that will remove all the pain and heartache, they should avoid the sufferer. Believing that they have nothing special to say, they don't communicate at all with the sufferer. And, then, there are some people who may fear that if they went to the afflicted person, the sufferer might break down and cry over what has happened. Not knowing how to deal with that if it should occur, the friend chooses to keep his or her distance.

However, remaining at a distance only confirms the worst fears of the person suffering. There is already the feeling of abandonment; the afflicted feels as though he or she has been given an enormous burden to bear for the rest of his or her life, and there will be no one to help. When family and friends keep their distance, they communicate that this apparently is true. The deeper fear is not just that one feels abandoned by family and friends, but that God is no longer there. It doesn't matter how much you have sensed God's presence before, for at times like this, he seems absent. And, when you know that God is the only one who can do anything about the problem, it is especially painful to sense his departure.

These emotions are also accompanied by anger. The anger may not be particularly rational, but it is nonetheless real. I was angry that this was happening to us. I never expected exemption from problems just because I am a Christian, but I never thought something like this would happen. In one fell stroke, we learned that my whole family was under a dark cloud of doom. That kind of catastrophe wasn't supposed to happen. I was angry.

Since I had known before I married that God wanted me in the ministry, had I known this about my wife's family, I probably wouldn't have married her. Pat has said that had she known, she probably wouldn't have married at all. If we had learned of her condition before starting a family, we wouldn't have had children. Any ethicist would say that it is morally dubious to subject someone to this fate if you know this could happen! I was angry at family members who knew and didn't tell us. I was angry at the doctors who knew and never explained it to the family. And I was angry at family members who didn't know even though they could have asked the doctors for an explanation. In short, if someone had told us the truth before we married, we could have avoided this terrible situation.

Though I didn't want to admit it, I was also angry at God. I knew that was foolish, because God hadn't done this. Nor could I think of anything in or out of Scripture that obligates God to keep things like this from happening. Beyond that, it was foolish to be angry with the only person who could do anything about this bleak situation. Anyway, who was I, the creature, to contest the Creator? As the apostle Paul says (Rom. 9:19–21), the creature has no right to haul the Creator into the courtroom of human moral judgments and put him on trial as though he has done something wrong. God has total power and authority over me. It is foolish to be angry with the One who has such total control over my every move.

Still, it is human nature to be angry and expect something different from God. There are questions about why we have to deal with this affliction when others don't. It's not that I would wish this disease on anyone else. Rather, the point is that others have escaped, so why shouldn't we as well? It just didn't seem fair that we had to bear this burden. In my case, my complaint wasn't just that God had allowed this to happen to us. I felt that God had somehow misled me, even tricked me. When Pat and I first met, we were sure there was no way we would marry. I was preparing for a teaching ministry in the United States, and she was headed to the mission field in Africa. Pat graduated from Nyack College and then applied to a number of mission boards to pursue her calling. However, no doors opened. She decided to go to Wheaton Grad School to do an MA in Christian Education. Another degree on her résumé would likely make her more attractive to mission boards, and she could surely use her training in Christian Ed on the mission field. In light of how God had led each of us to that point, it seemed impossible for this combination ever to work out. Our relationship grew, but I feared that we were in for disappointment if we continued, because it seemed God was leading us in different directions.

Before I met Pat I had been engaged to be married. In that case, I had clearly run ahead of the Lord. By God's grace I came to see that, and I broke off the engagement. But the experience emphasized how extremely careful I had to be in choosing a life partner. Above all, I had decided to seek and follow God's leading. It didn't pay to test God by continuing a relationship that seemed outside his will.

I sensed that I knew what Pat and I had to do. One night I went to break off the relationship. I was sure God wouldn't want us to defy his will to send us in different directions. I shared this with Pat and she agreed, but neither of us wanted it to end. At one point, I suggested that I would tell Pat what led me to believe God wanted me in a teaching ministry, and then she should tell me what had happened to cause her to believe that God wanted her in Africa. As Pat and I talked, we began to realize that she had a definite call to full-time ministry, but there was no clear call to foreign missions. We decided to pray independently about this whole thing, telling the Lord to break off the relationship (as painful as that would be), if he didn't want us together. We would do this for a month and then make a decision. In the meantime we continued to see each other; we just agreed not to talk about it until the month was over.

Rather than destroying the relationship, the Lord made it abundantly clear in various ways that he wanted us to marry. I'm sure many have heard stories of women who were called to the mission field, but fell in love with someone they met, married him instead, and never went into missions. As time passed, the marriage turned sour and the woman realized that God had definitely wanted her on the mission field; she had missed God's best for her life, and now she had nothing.

As common as such stories are, Pat talked with people who had stories with just the opposite result. She heard of women who believed God wanted them on the mission field. Before they went, however, they met someone and fell in love. Rather than marrying, they left their homeland to serve God in missions, believing that such was God's will. However, God hadn't really called them to missions, and the mission experience was a disaster. Before long they had to give up and return home. In the meantime, however, their prospective husband had married someone else. It was really God's will for these women to marry instead of go into missions, but they had misread God's direction for their life. Now they had nothing—no ministry and no husband.

So, Pat came to see that when given a choice between missions and marriage, choosing missions isn't always God's will. In addition, as Pat and I reflected on what was happening, we concluded that it was natural for her to think God wanted her in Africa. She had been very active in her home church and its youth group. The minister of youth had been a missionary to Africa, and he constantly spoke of the need for missionaries to go there. In such circumstances, it would be very natural for a teenager to conclude that she should become a missionary to Africa. In fact, God often does use our life circumstances to call us to one vocation or another. But, since there hadn't been any occasion when Pat had felt God's specific call to Africa, it seemed that the circumstances might be misleading her.

Through this whole process of talking to other Christians and reflecting on God's leading in her life (Pat was even able to talk with her former youth pastor about this—he and his family were living in Wheaton at the time) Pat became convinced that God wanted us to marry. And I was convinced, too. As I grew up, I often wondered if you could be sure that the person you marry is the right one. I figured that when the wedding day came around, you could be pretty sure you were marrying the right person, but not absolutely certain. That could only come after being married for a while and then seeing that you had chosen correctly. However, in light of how God had so clearly led us, I knew beyond a shadow of a doubt that God wanted me to marry Pat. Indeed, married life confirmed that.

I am still not certain whether most people, even if God does want them to marry, are certain on their wedding day that this is so. But I was absolutely certain, and I think God gave me that assurance in part because he knew that we would have to deal with Huntington's. With or without a clear sense of God's desire that we marry, we would eventually get the diagnosis of Huntington's Disease, anyway. But without being certain that God wanted me to marry Pat, I might have assumed that the disease was God's way of informing me that I really wasn't supposed to marry her. I had misread his will. Even more, Pat and I might see the disease as God's punishment on both of us for her not going to the mission field. By removing doubts before we married about what God wanted, God precluded such thoughts. Just because we have to deal with this disease, that's no reason for second-guessing whether God wanted us to marry each other.

With such certainty about God's leading in regard to our marriage, perhaps you can better understand why I felt I had been deceived. The Lord knew I was going into a very demanding ministry. He knew that I needed a wife to help me, and he knew that if I were really to give myself to the work he was giving me, I would need at least a relatively healthy wife. My Dad had a very fruitful ministry of the sort I envisioned. My Mom suffered with various physical problems, and I had seen the strain that had put on Dad. But Mom was never incapacitated to the point where she couldn't function in the home on a consistent basis. I reasoned that God knew all of that, so he would give me at least a relatively healthy wife. Of course, I assumed that the Lord would give me a certain kind of ministry. I couldn't see how I could have a wife with Pat's condition and carry on such a ministry. It didn't occur to me at the time that God might have in mind a different sort of ministry for me. So, if God were thinking what I was thinking, this shouldn't make sense to him either.

I was very confused, and the confusion came in part because the Lord had so clearly led us to marry. Besides, those who had been asked about whether Pat could have the same problems as her mother had assured us that there was nothing to worry about. Now I had learned the horrible truth, and I felt that I had been tricked. I had been led down a path, only to learn that I wasn't getting what I thought was.

I remember thinking repeatedly at the time that none of this made any sense. God is the supremely rational being, and yet it seemed that he was actualizing a contradiction in my life! The news of my wife's illness seemed to contradict the Lord's leading in my life over the previous fifteen years. I didn't know what to do, and I didn't even know what to think. At one point, I thought about Abraham. God had given him Isaac, the child of promise, only to tell him to sacrifice Isaac on Mt. Moriah. That must have made no more sense to Abraham than my situation made to me. Even so, Abraham had believed. He even believed that if he sacrificed Isaac, God would resurrect him from the dead (Heb. 11:19).

What incredible faith! I should be more like Abraham. Surely, his situation should comfort and encourage me. But it didn't. I remembered only too quickly that it made sense for Abraham to believe, because God had made very specific promises about this son (Gen. 12:1–3; 15:4–6; 17:15–19). God had made no such promises to me about my wife and children. He had made it clear that Pat and I should marry, and even saw to it that information likely to have kept us from marrying and having children was hidden. But he never promised that there would be no catastrophic illness. There had never been any promises about how long or how healthy a life any of us would have. Certainly, God could perform a miracle (as Abraham expected in Isaac's case) and heal the disease, but there were no guarantees that he would. As instructive as the example of Abraham and Isaac is, I had no right to take comfort from it.

I was also confused for another reason. I was raised around people who suffered greatly. As mentioned in chapter 1, my mother had one physical problem after another. I am sure that it was in part because of her experiences that I became interested at an early age in the problem of pain and suffering. As I grew up, I thought about the problem of evil repeatedly. In seminary, I wrote my Master of Divinity thesis on Job. Later, my Master of Theology thesis was devoted to God's sovereign control of all things and how that relates to human freedom. Then, my doctoral dissertation dealt with the problem of evil considered philosophically. If anyone had thought about this problem and was prepared to face real affliction, surely it was I. Yet when the events I have recounted occurred, I found little comfort in any of this intense intellectual reflection.

The truth is, I couldn't figure it out. I had all those intellectual answers, but none of them made any difference in how I felt on the personal level. As a professor of theology, surely I should understand what God was doing in this situation. On the contrary, I began wondering if in fact I really understood anything at all about God. The emotional and psychological pain was unrelenting, and the physical results from the stress and mental pain were devastating.

Why hadn't all the years of study, reflection, and writing on the problem of evil helped at this moment of personal crisis? I was experiencing a religious crisis, and none of this information I had stored away seemed to matter in the least. As I reflected on this, I came to what was for me a very significant realization. All my study and all the intellectual answers were of little help because the religious problem of evil (the problem about one's personal struggle with pain and suffering and how that affects one's relation to God) is not primarily an intellectual problem. Instead, it is fundamentally an emotional one! People wrestling with evil do not require an intellectual discourse on how to justify God's ways to his creation. Such answers address the more abstract theological and philosophical problems about why there should be any evil at all or evil in the amounts present in our world if there is a God. My problem, instead, was about how in the midst of affliction I could find comfort, and how I could find it in myself to live with this God who wasn't stopping the suffering.

This does not mean that no spiritual truths or intellectual answers can help the sufferer. It means that many of those answers won't help with this problem and others that do won't help at all stages in the sufferer's experience. They must be used at times when the emotional pain has healed enough so that they can make a difference.

At this point, I understood experientially that the religious problem of evil requires pastoral care rather than philosophical discussion. I can illustrate the point by a simple example.

Think of a little girl who goes out to play on a playground. Sometime during her play, she falls and skins her knee. She runs, screaming in pain, to her mother for comfort. Now, her mother can do any number of things. She may tell her daughter that this has happened because she was running too fast and wasn't watching where she was going; she must be more careful the next time. The mother might even explain (if she knew them) the laws of physics and causation that were operating to make her child's scrape just the size and shape it is. The mother might even expound for a few moments on the lessons God is trying to teach her child from this experience.

If the mother then asks her daughter if she understands, don't be surprised if the little girl responds, "Yes, Mommy, but it still hurts!" All the explanation at that moment doesn't stop her pain. The child doesn't want a discourse; she wants and needs her mother's hugs and kisses. There will be time for the discourse later; now she needs comfort.

The same is true for each of us as we struggle with the religious problem of evil. When the affliction first comes, we don't want or need a lengthy discourse to appeal to our mind, and that is so because this isn't primarily an intellectual matter. Even if you have something absolutely profound to say about the situation and you say it, don't be surprised if we are too hurt and confused to absorb it. We need someone to let us pour out our heart, not someone to give us a lecture, regardless of how brilliant and instructive it might be. And we need something to take away the pain, and a very big part of that pain is not knowing what these events mean about how God feels toward us. Or how we should feel toward him.

CHAPTER 3

RECIPES FOR DISASTER— OR HOW NOT TO HELP THE AFFLICTED

*I*f the religious problem of evil (the problem about personal struggles with pain and suffering) isn't primarily about justifying God's ways to man but about how to live with the God who doesn't stop the suffering, how can we help others through these difficult times in their life? I can only answer in terms of things that weren't helpful to me and things that did make a difference.

Invariably, people try to say something they hope will help. Sometimes it does, but often people can be extremely insensitive in the things they say or do, and this only drives the sufferer into further despair. No one means to do this; no one is trying to make the burden worse. Most just want to help. But despite good intentions, these would-be comforters often wind up doing more damage than good. Let me mention some things that are inappropriate to say and do.

"You Must Have Committed Some Sin"

Someone may say, "There must be some great sin you've committed; otherwise this wouldn't be happening to you."

I am very thankful that no one said this to me or my family, though it is a common reaction of some people when they hear of severe affliction. This was the reaction of many of Job's so-called comforters. They didn't really know what was happening, but they were sure it wouldn't look good for God if a righteous man suffered. Therefore, they reasoned that God would only allow this to happen to the guilty.

While it is true that God punishes sin, and that the wicked will have a day of judgment, Scripture is very clear that sometimes the ungodly do prosper (Ps. 73), while the righteous suffer (Job 1:8; 2:3; 1 Pet. 4:12–19). The truth is that in most instances we don't really know whether someone suffers as a righteous person or as a sinner. Outwardly moral people may be great sinners, and even those who seem righteous may be guilty of some hidden sin. The story of the rich man and Lazarus (Luke 16) is a vivid reminder that outward appearances don't provide a good basis for judging spirituality. If someone is truly suffering in punishment for sin, that person will likely know it without our saying a thing. If that person doesn't realize it, it is still probably better to ask him what he thinks God is saying through the affliction, rather than offering our opinion that he must have committed some sin. If someone is suffering for righteousness' sake, as was Job, it definitely won't help if those who aren't suffering assume an attitude of moral superiority and accuse the sufferer of sin.

Things vs. People

Another mistake is to focus on the loss of things rather than the loss of people. I do not speak from personal experience, but from that of a relative. Some years ago this relative was on vacation. While away, she learned that her home had burned to the ground, trapping and killing her son who was unable to escape. Her pastor tried to be of help, but made some significant mistakes in handling the situation. For one thing, he made very little attempt to see her and allow her to talk out her feelings. The few times he did say something, he expressed concern over the loss of her house and possessions. You can imagine how hurt she was. The loss of one's home and possessions is not insignificant, but in one way or another, most of those things can be replaced. The loss of a loved one is the greatest loss one can suffer, for how does one replace a son? That pastor completely missed the point of her grief. By his insensitivity, he missed the opportunity to minister to her in her time of crisis, and hindered rather than helped the healing process.

Talking vs. Listening

In chapter 2, I mentioned that when tragedy strikes, friends often leave the afflicted alone, because they are afraid that they will say something wrong to make the situation worse. Or they may fear that they won't have something profound to say that will relieve the pain. All of this underscores a basic misjudging of what the sufferer really needs. When tragedy first strikes, and for a long time after, the bereaved need some way to express all the thoughts and feelings they are experiencing. They long to have someone who cares enough just to listen to them pour out their heart. Though it is natural to want to say something that will relieve the sufferer's pain, it is even more important that we listen to what they want to say.

In the weeks and months following Pat's diagnosis, I had so many thoughts and emotions rushing through my mind that I felt like there was a war going on inside my head. I felt like I would explode if I couldn't share what I was feeling. I needed to express my thoughts, but I found few who would listen. I don't think friends and acquaintances didn't really care. I just think they weren't sure what to expect if they listened and whether they might make things worse by saying the wrong thing in response to what I would say. It was easier to pray for us or to offer a word of concern than to listen. Even today there are times when I just need someone to listen to how I feel and to what I've been thinking. And this is why it is so important for us to "be there" to listen, even if we have nothing profound to say in response. At times of crises our profoundest contribution is our presence and our open ears. It says that we care and we understand the need to make public what is going on inside our head and our heart.

So don't avoid the afflicted out of fear that you don't have the "magic words" to make the pain go away. Even if you have those words, when the pain is new and so intense, the sufferer cannot process what you would say. By listening instead, you gain the right to be heard when the sufferer is really ready and able to listen. Those who won't listen when listening is needed communicate either that they don't care about what the sufferer is feeling and thinking, or that they have the ready answer to the problem and thus what has happened must not be all that bad. They communicate that they don't really understand or fully appreciate what the sufferer is experiencing.

In the Book of Job, I think we see these points vividly illustrated. Job's friends made a lot of mistakes in "ministering" to his needs, but there was one thing they did that was exactly what he needed. After the second wave of afflictions, Job's friends came to comfort him, and they sat with him for seven days and nights. *And they said nothing.* Scripture says that they didn't speak to him because they saw that his grief was very great (Job 2:13). This showed great sensitivity to how he was feeling and to what would most help him. We are not told what Job said or did during those seven days and nights. But surely his friends were right to be there and to be quiet! The "trouble" only began when they opened their mouths, attempting to soothe his grief by "dumping" upon him a load of speculations about why this had happened and what he should do to relieve his pain.

God's timing in responding to Job also illustrates this point. Job repeatedly sought God and expressed his wish to plead his case before God. "Oh, that I knew where I might find him," says Job, "that I might come even to his seat! I would set my case before him, and fill my mouth with arguments" (Job 23:3–4). Yet God remained silent.

God could have spoken the words recorded in chapters 38–41 shortly after Job's afflictions began, but he didn't. Some may reply that if God's answer had come immediately after chapter 2, it would ruin the literary impact of the book. Only after we read the many chapters of dialogue between Job and his friends are we ready to hear God's answer. I would not discount this point about the literary form of dialogue or about the impact of placing these chapters where the author did. But there is no indication that this is a fictional story so that the author could have imagined the events in any sequence that would fit his literary agenda. Instead, the author is telling us that God really waited a long time before he answered Job.

And that makes abundant sense, for surely God knows our nature far better than we do. Thus, he knew that what Job needed was time and opportunity to express his feelings, his questions, and his doubts. And so he kept silent, listening to Job vent his thoughts and emotions. God is too wise to think that had he spoken the words of chapters 38–41 right after the afflictions fell, Job would have been ready to hear and process them. It is only after Job has repeatedly thought through his situation and stated his feelings again and again that he is ready to hear God's reply. And so God waited, listening, not speaking. We would be wise to do the same as we minister to the afflicted.

Job wanted to find God so that he could plead his case before him. Though Job didn't sense it, God was actually there all the time, listening to Job and his friends. And he is present in our lives when we experience the pain of tragedy. We wish that he would explain why this is happening to us, but God listens to our expressions of grief, waiting until just the moment when we are ready to hear him, before he answers us.

In my case, I needed listeners. Friends who listened to me ministered much more than I realized at the time. I can't imagine how much harder this experience would have been if no one at all had listened. One of those who did listen was a professional counselor. I remember that I had certain expectations about what would happen in the sessions with him. I didn't expect him to answer all my theological and philosophical questions about what was happening. But I did expect him to tell me what to do to move beyond the deep grief I was feeling. Much to my surprise (and, to a certain extent, frustration), he said very little in any of our sessions, especially the early ones. He asked an occasional question to keep me talking about my thoughts and feelings, but he offered little advice or commentary.

Early on, I thought that the sessions were somewhat a waste of time for him and me, because I was taking from them so little that seemed helpful. On the other hand, I thought to myself that at least now I was getting a chance to lay out in detail piece by piece my thoughts and feelings about what was happening. And even if he had little advice to offer, at least getting the chance to say what I was thinking was good. As the sessions continued, the counselor did begin to give some advice, and I found it helpful. Because he had listened so patiently to me, how could I not listen carefully to him? Moreover, I knew that whatever advice he offered was given from the vantage point of one who had a thorough knowledge of what I was thinking and feeling. There would be little need to "counter" what he said by adding elements of my story that might change his advice. He already knew many of the details because he had listened so well.

I have devoted much space to this point, because I think it so important. Listening alone won't make the pain go away completely, but it is a key first step. But my main reason for giving so much attention to this matter is that I hope it will encourage readers not to abandon the sufferer. I hope that you will see that even if you don't have something to say that will remove the pain, you should still go to your suffering friend or family member. Just listening is more helpful than you can ever imagine!

"This Has Probably Spared You from Worse Problems"

Sometimes when we lose a loved one, people try to comfort us by convincing us that what has happened is for the best because it spares us from other problems. Here I relate the experience of one of my students. This student and his wife had their first baby, and he was in my class for the term just after the baby's birth. About midway through the term, the baby died very suddenly. After the funeral and toward the end of the term, he shared with the class some of what he had learned. Part of what he told us focused on things not to say to someone experiencing such grief. He told us how some people had said, "You know, it's probably a good thing that your son died. He probably would have grown up to be a problem. Maybe he'd have been a drug addict or would have refused to follow Christ. God knows these things in advance, and he was probably just saving you from those problems."

I trust that no one thinks this is an appropriate thing to say. It may be true that the child *would* have been a problem, but it is hard to see how that information is a comfort at the time of loss. Parents and other relatives love that child, and they love him regardless of whether or not he was or would have been a problem. Their loss is extremely painful, and the pain is not eased, let alone removed, by insensitive speculations about the future. Moreover, the comment is wrong, because it in effect says that it is good that evil has happened. I don't see how that can ever be an appropriate attitude for a Christian. Yes, James says we are to count it all joy when we fall into various afflictions (James 1:1–2), but we must not misunderstand this. The affliction isn't joy; it is evil. The cause for joy is that in spite of the evil, God is with us and can accomplish positive things in our life even in the midst of affliction. But the affliction isn't a good thing. If it were, we might be inclined to seek suffering. Obviously, nothing in Scripture suggests that we should do that. Anyway, we don't have to seek affliction; it has a way of finding us.

"Just Remember Romans 8:28"

It is not unusual for some well-meaning person to see us suffering and offer the following advice. "I can see this is quite a struggle for you. But just remember that in Romans 8:28 God promises that 'all things work together for good.'" Though quoting Scripture to the afflicted can be a good strategy, quoting this passage is not necessarily helpful, for a number of reasons.

For one thing, those who understand what you are saying usually remember that there is more to the verse. Paul says that this will happen to "those who love God, who have been called according to his purpose." It is not unlikely that reminding sufferers of this verse will stir up in them a variety of doubts. They may reason, "Since all things work together for good for those who love God and are called according to his purpose, maybe the reason that this is happening and hasn't yet turned out for good is that my love for God isn't what it should be. Or maybe God has his will and purposes for me, but I'm out of his will, and that's why this has happened. In fact, maybe by quoting this verse my friend is implicitly accusing me of those problems."

Surely, such doubts in no way help the sufferer. The would-be comforter of course doesn't intend to make the burden heavier by adding such a burden of doubt and guilt. However, there are other problems with quoting this verse. Clearly, Paul is appealing to the ability of a sovereign God to turn everything that happens to believers, even adversity, into something profitable for them. But in light of verses 29 and 30, which explain why verse 28 is true, it is clear that the good envisioned here pertains to the believer's salvation, not just anything that contributes to worldly convenience or comfort. Paul writes: "For those God foreknew he also predestined to be conformed to the likeness of his Son, that he might be the firstborn among many brothers. And those he predestined, he also called; those he called, he also justified; those he justified, he also glorified."

Nonetheless, those who quote this verse often think it guarantees a life of ease and convenience. If it doesn't, it is simply misleading to quote this verse as though it means that the afflicted should feel better because God will soon restore all things we lost that made life easy and convenient for us. That is surely not the verse's point.

There is a third problem with reminding the sufferer of Romans 8:28, especially if one uses it at early stages of the sufferer's affliction. The problem is that it again treats what is primarily an emotional problem as though it is only an intellectual one. We think that if we can just get the sufferer the "right" information, all the pain will just go away. If the mother of the little girl who skinned her knee quoted Romans 8:28 to her daughter, would that remove the pain? Of course not, and not just because she's a little girl!

Do not misunderstand this. There will be a time in the sufferer's experience when it will be helpful to offer this and other biblical and theological information in an attempt to comfort. But when emotional and physical pain are so severe, don't expect the sufferer's mind to be functioning at full speed. Even if it is, the right information won't remove the pain!

There are two other problems with quoting this verse, and I think these are the most significant. For one thing, at the point in our suffering when someone quotes this verse, God typically hasn't brought good out of this evil. Often those who suffer can't see how or when God will do so. Reminding them of what God can do before God has done anything isn't likely to help very much.

In addition, it is hard to see how that good, whenever it comes and whatever it will be, will make up for the evil that has happened. Surely, the would-be comforter does not mean to say that evil which has happened is really all right because eventually God will overrule this adversity to do something good. Moreover, I hope that by quoting this verse no one is suggesting that since God will turn things to good, even the evil that has happened isn't really evil! Unfortunately, quoting

Romans 8:28 may just give the sufferer such false impressions. How insensitive to imply that a tragedy of a lost loved one, or some other tragedy, really isn't that bad or that it isn't even evil at all, because God will eventually bring something good out of the experience! God used the murder of Jesus Christ on Calvary to purchase our salvation, but that doesn't make our Lord's death any less a murder, nor does it mean that those who put him to death deserve praise as moral heroes!

Remember that even Jesus wept when Lazarus died (John 11:35). The fact that Jesus had power to raise his friend from the dead (and did so) didn't cause Jesus to think that what had happened was trivial. Jesus knew this was a terrible evil, and so he wept, even though he knew he could raise Lazarus from the dead. Scripture also tells us that as a result of sin, the whole creation was subjected to futility (Rom. 8:20). The fact that God will someday reverse the curse placed on creation (Rom. 8:21) in no way minimizes the evil that has happened. God's overturning the results of sin in our world and using that to demonstrate his glory and power don't mean the sin was good. After all, God told the human race he didn't want us to sin. The fact that he can display his mighty and gracious hand in saving sinners does not mean he is actually happy that we sinned, making his salvation possible, or that sin is not really sin!

Things happen in our world that really *are* evil! Don't minimize that fact by appealing to the sovereign ability of God to bring good even out of the most horrible situation. Somewhere down the road, after the sufferer's pain has somewhat subsided and there has been time to see what God will do in the midst of the tragedy, maybe then it will be a comfort to remind the sufferer of this verse. Don't be surprised if the afflicted person has already recited that verse many times over. Regardless of what good God has brought out of the evil situation, that doesn't mean the evil isn't really evil! And quoting this verse, true though it is, won't make the pain go away!

"We're All Going to Die Someday"

There are other comments that don't help. Not long after we learned the truth about my wife's condition, someone said this to me: "Well, you know, everyone's going to die from something. You just know in advance what it is in your wife's case."

Even if this were true, how can it be a comfort? Does the thought of your own death bring you comfort? If you knew in advance the *cause* of your own death, would you be inclined to say, "Ah, well, very good; now I can rest easy knowing what will get me"? No one likes to reflect on their own or a loved one's demise. That it will happen to all of us is no encouragement, nor is knowing the manner of our death. That is true even if ours will be an "easy death," not to mention facing death from a catastrophic disease. At the time of someone's grief, do not think you will help them by reminding them we will all die someday, or that at least they know in advance how they will die.

The other problem with this comment is that it is not necessarily true—that is, that we can ever know for certain in advance the cause of our death. Indeed, the likelihood that my wife will die of Huntington's Disease is great, but it isn't absolutely certain. She could die of a heart attack, in a car accident, or some other way. None of that is cause for rejoicing either, but it does show that the comment in question is neither helpful nor necessarily correct.

Furthermore, it doesn't help to remind me or my wife that despite her disease and despite the fact that it takes people when they are relatively young, I might still die before she does. That could also be true, but I don't find it comforting to think that at a time when Pat is least able to function and most in need of my help, I might not be there. That doesn't encourage her either.

"Don't Think About Any Major Changes"

When the doctor first diagnosed Pat's condition, he told her some things that he must have thought would be helpful. After giving the diagnosis, he said, "Well, you better think about it long and hard before having any more children. And, you and your husband better not think about changing jobs. If you do, you might not be able to get health insurance."

I am confident that her physician meant well and wanted to be helpful. Indeed, we needed to think about these things. But, there is a time to be told such things, and right at the outset is not it. Earlier I described the feelings of abandonment and hopelessness. Along with those feelings is the sense that one is trapped in the situation and helpless to escape. What that doctor said in no way helped to alleviate those feelings. On the contrary, it confirmed our feelings of entrapment. While I love my job and where I'm doing it, nobody likes to feel that their life's options are being limited or cut off, especially when they face seemingly insurmountable problems.

Yes, we needed that information, but not at that time. When someone you know gets shocking news, they are in need of some practical advice about their situation. However, timing is crucial. I would encourage you to be ultra-sensitive to their feelings. At the moment when they are feeling totally devastated by the news, don't add to their misery by telling them things that will only add to their feelings of entrapment and abandonment. If you feel you must say something, it would probably be better just to encourage them not to make any major decisions until they have had some time to sort things out. But they probably know that already!

"I Know How You Feel"

One of the most typical things people say is something I have said myself at times when visiting the sick or the bereaved. As we fumble for something to share that will comfort our friend or loved one, somehow it seems appropriate to say "I know how you must feel at a time like this." Through my experiences, I have learned how inappropriate and unhelpful this comment can be. The problem is really twofold. On the one hand, it isn't true, and the sufferer knows it. Hence, it sounds phony when you say it. Even if you think you know how I feel, and even if the same thing happened to you, you still don't know how I feel and you can't know how I feel. You can't because you are not me with my particular personality and emotions, with my background and experiences, with my family and the relations we share with one another. Nor can I know exactly how *you* feel when suffering comes your way. Telling me that you know how I feel sounds like an insincere and cheap way to try to comfort me. I know it can't be true.

If something similar has indeed happened to you, you may tell me this because you think I might be encouraged by hearing that others have suffered greatly and yet have survived. If that is your point, then just say that, rather than saying you know how I feel. What you say may still not comfort me, because I may be in too much pain at the time to think I'll ever make it through the particular crisis at hand. You can say this from the vantage point of looking back at your own crisis and seeing that you survived. But remember that I am still in the midst of my crisis. Your experience is no guarantee that I'll make it.

While your reassurance that you and others have survived tragedy may not comfort me, at least that comment is true. You aren't telling me you know how I feel when I know you can't know how I feel. You are simply saying that though these things are hard, others like yourself have experienced tragedy and still survived. Unless I am totally different from everyone else, it is possible for me to make it, too.

The other problem with saying you know how I feel is that it really doesn't matter whether you know how I feel. For one thing, do you think I would rejoice in knowing that you feel as miserable as I do? I wouldn't wish my feelings of grief on my enemies, let alone my friends. To know that you feel as bad as I do would make me feel worse, not better. Beyond that, the fundamental reason it doesn't matter whether or not you know how I feel is that this information alone won't help me. What helps is not knowing you feel like I do, but knowing that you care!

Look at it this way. Suppose some horrible tragedy happened to you. Suppose I had experienced the same thing, and suppose I know you. Suppose I tell you, "You know, I know exactly how you feel. I've been there myself. But you know what? While I know how you feel, I don't really care about what's happening to you."

Would that comfort or help you? Of course not! However, if I tell you I *don't* know how you feel, but I *do* care, and I want to be of help, that will make a difference. It will especially help if your words are followed by tangible deeds that show you are serious about helping. Remember, those who suffer feel help-less, hopeless, and abandoned. They need us to care and to show that care by helping however we can. *They don't need us to share their feelings; they need us to share their burdens!*

Here I must also add that it doesn't really help to tell me that Jesus knows how I feel, because he suffered greatly during his earthly pilgrimage. Or that God knows how I feel about losing Pat, because he watched his Son die on Calvary. I take no comfort from any of that. Rather my reaction is: "Oh great! Just what we need—more victims! This is definitely not a time when misery wants company!" The fact that God himself has suffered because of the sin of the human race in no way encourages or comforts me. It reminds me of my part in making his suffering necessary, and that only makes me feel worse.

I have found 1 Peter 5:7 to be a very helpful passage. But it is important to see what this familiar passage doesn't say as well as what it does. Peter could have written, "Cast all your cares upon him, because he has suffered, too, and knows how you feel." I find that statement to be nowhere near as encouraging as what Peter did write. Peter tells us to cast our cares on Christ, because he *cares* for us. That's the key. Not someone to feel as bad as we do, but someone who cares about our troubles and is there to help carry our burdens!

In all of this, it is very important to recognize the difference between "I know how you feel" and "I really feel for you." The former identifies with the sufferer. The latter shows we care.

"If You'd Just Change Your View of God, Everything Would Be Fine"

The months wore on after my wife's diagnosis, and as already mentioned in this chapter, I longed to have someone to talk to about how I felt. Before I went to the Christian counselor a dear, godly colleague who has been a friend for many years offered to listen. I began to explain how perplexed I was by what had happened. It seemed that God hid information from us about my wife prior to our marriage, and again prior to our having children. I noted that with my Calvinistic conception of God, where God controls all things, this was especially troublesome. Even if I were more inclined toward an Arminian notion of God, where God takes a less-active role in the world to leave more room for human freedom, it still seemed to me that God should have intervened in our behalf. After all, hadn't we prayed that the Lord would lead us and keep us from making a wrong decision about whether to marry? My friend replied that I was talking about this concept of God and that model of God. What I really needed to do was stop such talk and recognize that God is bigger than all our conceptions of him.

There is something very right about what my friend said. Surely, we can never hope to understand our majestic and mighty God thoroughly through human thought forms. Yet I found my friend's comments unhelpful. For one thing, he failed to see that his comment about God being bigger than all our conceptions of him is itself another conception of God.

However, the real problem was that my friend in essence was saying that things would be better for me if I just changed my ideas about God. Now, it is true that sufferers who are atheists need to change their perception of God. A Christian who has little training in theology might also need a better understanding of the nature and attributes of God. In fact, even theology professors could hardly be hurt by adjusting their views to a more accurate picture of God.

But even though this is true, there is still a major problem in thinking that this will resolve the religious problem of evil. What is wrong with telling someone in this situation that all they really need to do is just change their view of God? The problem is that this treats a fundamentally emotional problem as if it were an intellectual problem. Please do not misunderstand this. The afflicted *may* have a wrong concept of God, and at some point in dealing with them, we must help them get a better picture of what God is like. On the other hand, if the religious problem is, as I suggest, at root an emotional hurt, that must be handled first. You don't handle an emotional problem by telling someone to adjust their idea of God. You can change your view of God and still find that the pain remains!

There are other forms of this error that are just as common among Christians. One is, "You know, if you were a Calvinist, you'd see that God is in control of all of this, and then you could rest in him." Another is, "You know, if you weren't so Calvinistic, you wouldn't think God has his hand so directly in everything, and then you'd stop blaming him for what's happened to you." Perhaps the most common is, "When things like this happen, aren't you glad you're a Calvinist? Isn't it great to know that God is ultimately in control of it all, and that he's already planned the way out of your problem?"

The first two of these comments are really saying that this whole thing will be all right if you just change your view of God. We have already talked about this mistake. The third comment doesn't tell sufferers to get a new concept of God but rather tells them to take comfort in their beliefs about God. Don't assume, though, that this will in fact comfort everyone. I am a Calvinist, and I found this comment distressing, not helpful. Because of my belief in God's control over all things, and because it appeared that God had misled me, I took no comfort in the fact that I was a Calvinist. In fact, I remember thinking quite frequently that everything that had happened to me and my family would be easier to take if I were an Arminian. At least then I wouldn't see God so actively and directly in control of what had happened.

What was the problem here? Was it that I really needed to discard my Calvinism as inadequate? Not at all. Had I been an Arminian, what had happened would still hurt terribly. The problem was that others who made the comment, and I as well, thought this deep emotional wound could be salved by simply reflecting on this intellectual concept. Indeed, there is a time for explanation and reflection upon what one knows to be true of God. If one's ideas about God are wrong, there is also a time for changing them. But not when the hurt is so deep and so new!

Remember the little girl with the skinned knee. In answer to her mother's explanations she says, "Yes, Mommy, but it still hurts." This is not a problem that requires philosophical or theological discourse; it requires pastoral care. In any given case, no one can predict how long it will take for the pain to subside to the point where the sufferer is ready to think seriously about concepts of God. You can be sure, however, that until it does, it won't help the afflicted to tell them to change their view of God or simply meditate on what they believe about him.

"You Aren't Spiritually Mature Unless You're Happy About This"

There was one other thing I found unhelpful in the midst of this emotional and spiritual turmoil and upheaval. I was concerned about my response to our situation, and I felt guilty that I wasn't on top of things. After all, Christians are supposed to rejoice in all things and persevere no matter what. Beyond that, as one in a position of Christian leadership, people would be looking all the more closely at me to see how I handled this. Still, I was finding it hard to cope. I preach quite frequently, but for about six months I was physically, emotionally, and spiritually unable to do so. I felt that anything I would say would be hypocritical because I wasn't living whatever I might preach.

All of this was disturbing enough, but my uneasiness increased. One day I was listening to a Christian radio program. A husband and wife who had lost a daughter in her twenties in an automobile accident were giving their testimony. They recounted what had happened to their daughter and how, as a result of these events, various people had come to know the Lord. They concluded that even though the loss of their daughter was hard, it was all for the best. It was good that this had happened.

I heard that and I felt more guilty. It seemed the height of Christian maturity to take life's harshest blows and say that it was good that this had happened. If that's what it means to be victorious in the midst of affliction, I knew I was far from that. I couldn't rejoice over the evil that had befallen and would befall my family. But wasn't I supposed to? After all, doesn't Paul tell us to "give thanks in all circumstances, for this is God's will for you in Christ Jesus" (1 Thess. 5:18)? My sense of inadequacy increased.

What my friend and colleague said on this matter was most helpful. I told him I knew I was supposed to respond Christianly in this situation. Did that mean, though, that I had to like what was happening? Without batting an eyelash he responded, "You do have to learn to live with this, but that doesn't mean you have to like it!"

This may sound like heresy to some. Popular Christian belief reminds us to rejoice in everything and count it all joy when trials come our way. One is not really "with it" spiritually without being able to say that the affliction is a good thing—or so we are told. I beg to differ. Thinking that way won't help us to cope with our grief; it will only add to it as we feel guilty about our inability to do what we think we are called to do.

My friend was right, and I came to see why as I reflected on this over the following weeks and months. First Thessalonians 5:18 is often misread. Paul does not say that we are to give thanks *for* everything, but *in* everything (that is, in the midst of everything). The affliction is evil, not good. Why should I thank God for evil? Furthermore, James 1:2–4 does not say that affliction is good or that it is a cause for rejoicing. It says that we are to rejoice when these things happen because God is sufficient in the midst of trials. We are to rejoice when we face trials because we can see what God is accomplishing *in spite of* the trial. Affliction may serve as the occasion for God to do good things in our life, but the suffering is not good. It is still evil.

Because the affliction is evil, I am not required to like it. All of us have sinned, and so we live in a fallen world. That is why it is even possible for these things to happen. Scripture is very clear that people die because of sin (Rom. 5:12). If people are going to die, they must die from something, and many will die from diseases that take life. Unless Jesus Christ returns for his church before we die, all of us will die as a consequence of living in a fallen world. Please do not misunderstand this. I am not suggesting that the reason Pat has Huntington's Disease is that she is a much worse sinner than others and this is her just recompense. On the contrary, I would contend that she is far more godly than most people I have ever known. My point is that all of us have sinned, and hence we are all responsible for the fallen world in which we live.

If disease and death are ultimately the consequences of living in a sinful, fallen world, how can I applaud it? As a Christian, I am called to resist sin and its consequences in all forms. How, then, can I exult when the consequences of sin befall anyone, let alone a loved one? No, we don't have to like it, and if we properly understand the ultimate cause of disease and death, we had better not like it!

It is wrong in another respect to suggest that the sufferer give thanks for suffering. It is wrong because it ignores our humanness. Grief and sorrow in the face of tragedy are very human emotions. Unless they are admitted and expressed, they will remain inside us and destroy us. Healing can't come if we deny what we are feeling and act as though it is good that evil has occurred. Those negative feelings must be admitted and expressed. They must be dealt with, not hidden so that the sufferer *acts* as though everything is all right. We can't help the afflicted if we expect them to deny their humanness.

Realizing that I didn't have to like what was happening relieved a great burden. Other things helped me as well. In the next chapter I turn from things that didn't help to those that did. The things I'll mention didn't all happen at once, and in some cases it took a while after they occurred for their import to sink in. If you are wrestling with the religious problem, I trust that you will read these comments with that in mind. None of it may help you now, but don't hesitate to come back to part or all of it later.

CHAPTER 4

THE GOODNESS OF GOD

Though many things didn't help me, others did. One thing that did help over time came in a conversation with my father several weeks after we first received my wife's diagnosis. I was bemoaning the fact that things looked so hopeless. I couldn't see how I would be able to handle it as Pat got worse. On top of that, there was the prospect of having to go through the same thing with one or more of our children. I didn't know how I would take it. At that point Dad said, "John, God never promised to give you tomorrow's grace for today. He only promised today's grace for today, and that's all you need!"

How true that is! In that one comment I was reminded both of God's grace and of my need to take each day one at a time. God has impressed upon me the fact that I don't have to live my tomorrows today. I don't know how I'll cope when my tomorrows come, but I know that they will come only one day at a time, and with each day, even as now, there will be grace to meet each new challenge—for me and my wife. That doesn't mean it will be fun, but it does mean that for each day God will provide the strength needed.

I have always been a goal-oriented person with an eye to planning for the future. As a result of this truth about grace, I began to readjust my focus from the future to the present.

I would begin each day asking God for just the grace needed to sustain me that day. As that prayer was answered day after day, I gained more assurance that God would be there when things got worse. As a result, I found that I worried less about the future, and focused more on the present day and its responsibilities. I still think about and plan for the future, but increasingly as Pat's condition worsens, I think in terms of the near future.

Often people ask me whether I am member of a Huntington's Disease support group. Some of them have addresses, phone numbers, and e-mail information to help me get involved. I know that such groups can be very helpful and that they are truly a lifeline for many families. However, I am not in such a group, and that is by choice. My personality is such that if I saw other Huntington's patients and heard them and their families talk about their challenges, I would likely project their symptoms and struggles on Pat and me. That would not be wise at all. While there is a group of symptoms associated with Huntington's Disease, no one can predict which symptoms will afflict each person, nor is it clear how long any symptom will last or how severe it will be. Because of the nature of this disease—and it has even taken an unpredictable path in Pat's case—I can see no reason to worry about symptoms she might never have. Jesus told us not to worry about tomorrow's problems today (Matt. 6:34), and that makes abundant sense. I don't have tomorrow's grace now, so I'm not ready for its problems either. And I especially shouldn't worry about tomorrow's problems when those challenges may never include symptoms other Huntington's patients have. So while being in a support group works well for others, I took a different path.

Another major factor in helping me to cope, though I didn't realize it at the time, was seeing that God and others really do care. I spoke earlier of the sense of abandonment and helplessness one feels. There is a sense that an incredible burden has been put on one's shoulders, and no one is there to help carry it. In the midst of those feelings, God used various people to show me that he and others knew what my wife and I were going through—and that they cared.

Several incidents in particular were especially meaningful. Shortly after the news came about Pat, my brother came to encourage me. I remember him saying that though I might feel abandoned at that moment, God hadn't abandoned me, and neither had he or the rest of my family. At that point I was still in such shock that I didn't recognize I was actually feeling a sense of abandonment. But God knew it and sent my brother to reassure me.

I also remember an important visit from my pastor. No one told him to visit us, and we hadn't asked that he come. He knew we were hurting, and he cared enough to do something. I remember well the first thing he said to me. He told me that he couldn't begin to know how I felt, but he wanted me to know that he really cared about what was happening, and that he and the church wanted to help in any way possible. I didn't realize it, but I really needed to hear that. He didn't say much more, but he was willing to be there and listen. His presence said he cared. At a time when it seems impossible to survive the grief and when everything appears hopeless, we need to know that someone cares and will help.

There were other visits, and words were matched with actions. My pastor noticed that our home was in need of some decorating. He took it upon himself to get together a group of people from the church to do it. It was their way of saying they loved us, were sorry about what had happened, and wanted to do something tangible to express that love. Some might think this was a strange thing for them to do. After all, how could painting some rooms help with this catastrophic disease? On the contrary, however, what they did struck me as God's way of showing me that if these people cared enough to do this, they and others would also be there when I needed more involved help to care for my wife.

People feel so bad about what is happening, and they just wish they could do something tangible to express their love and concern. Let them do things like my church friends did. It will be good for them and for you! As Pat's condition deteriorates and she is able to do less, Christian friends and acquaintances are still there showing in various ways that they care. What a beautiful picture of God's love for us!

What my pastor and church did in our home illustrates another point about caring for the afflicted. Often when we hear of someone in need, we tell them, "If there's anything I can do to be of help, just let me know." This expresses concern, but think about what you have just done.

On top of all the grief and pain the sufferer is feeling, you've just given them an assignment—devote some of your emotional and mental energy to thinking about something I can do for you. We can be smarter than this, can't we? We know that groceries need to be bought, children need to be taken to music lessons and team practices, lawns need to be mowed, and rooms need painting. Why not tell the afflicted, "I know Jimmy has baseball practice this afternoon, and I'd be happy to see that he gets there and back." Or, "I'm going to the grocery store this morning; can I pick you up some fruit that's on a special sale now and some other groceries?" Or, "I can see that you have rooms in your home that haven't been painted in a long time. Let me organize a group of friends to come and do that for you."

All of these imagined comments have at least one thing in common. They mention a specific need and a way that you would be happy to fill it. When you put things this way, rather than offering unspecific help in general, the sufferer knows that you really would like to do this. If you just offer help in general, the afflicted may be afraid to ask for something specific because it might not be something you'd really like to do or be able to do. Still, having offered, they'd be obligated to do it, even if they didn't want to. Knowing such things, my reaction when someone offers help in general is not to ask for anything, since I don't want to burden anyone with something they'd rather not do. But if you offer to do something specific, it saves me the time and effort of having to think up something you can do for me. Plus, if I agree to let you do this, I know I'm not asking you to do something you can't or don't want to do. Moreover, your offer of something specific, as my pastor did, tells me that you really do care and are attentive to my specific situation. That alone, not to mention the specific help you actually give me, encourages me greatly!

Not only have people at my church been helpful and caring, but so have colleagues and students at Trinity Evangelical Divinity School where I teach. After Pat was first diagnosed, students on their own initiative set aside special times each week to pray for us. Students and colleagues still pray for us, and many in the Trinity community express their concern by asking periodically how we are doing and by offering help.

The administration at Trinity over the years has been wonderful in working with us and our situation. It was difficult for me to teach many of my classes for a long time after we received the news of Pat's Huntington's Disease. Rather than scolding me or threatening to remove me from my teaching assignments, those in administration responded with patience and understanding. I was scheduled for a sabbatical that first academic year when the news came, and I was supposed to work on some writing projects. I was in such physical pain, let alone emotional stress, that I didn't know how I would be able to write during my sabbatical. I mentioned this to the president and dean, suggesting that perhaps I should postpone the leave. They took a more compassionate approach. The president and board told me to take the quarter off, and to consider it a combination sabbatical and medical leave of absence. I was told not to worry about how much writing I would accomplish. Though I did in fact get much done that sabbatical, that didn't overshadow their care, concern, and compassion toward me at such a difficult time.

As Pat's needs have grown and I have had to devote more time and attention to her care, Trinity's administration has been wonderfully gracious and helpful to us. They have willingly adjusted my schedule and responsibilities so that I can continue to minister at Trinity, and do so in a way that leaves me time to attend to Pat's needs.

All these events and many more have convinced me that there are people who actually care and will stand with us as Pat's condition becomes worse. I also view these acts of kindness as God's sign that he cares as well. All of this ministered to me greatly and helped to overcome the feelings of abandonment, hopelessness, and helplessness. And I know who sends people to help us; God's care for us shines through the helpful deeds of others!

There is part of our story that I have only mentioned in passing, but it is worth elaborating in relation to this point about caring for the afflicted. In earlier chapters I mentioned my mother-in-law's chart from the hospital in New York where she spent the last decade of her life. Because she had died ten

years before Pat's diagnosis and because of our need to confirm
or disconfirm the diagnosis in Pat's case, the hospital sent us
the chart.

When the chart came, I began to look through it. My
mother-in-law had been admitted to that hospital in 1967,
five years before my wife and I met and married. As I read the
chart, I didn't understand much of it, but one thing I saw horrified me. Within a few months of her arrival at the hospital,
the diagnosis of Huntington's Disease was recorded in her
chart. The information that could have saved us from this situation was there for five years before I even met my wife. The
information that could have kept us from having children and
saddling them with this burden was right there from 1967
onward. It had been there for twenty years, and no one told us
about it, even though we sought answers. When we finally did
learn the truth, it wasn't from that chart.

When I saw that information, I was furious. You can see
why I was so angry and why I felt so cheated and misled. You
can understand as well why comments about it being great to
be a Calvinist at a time like this didn't comfort me, but
repulsed me.

In the months and years that have passed since that reve-
lation, I have come to see this in a different way. For twenty
years that information was there, and at any time we could
have found it out. Why, then, did God not give it to us until
1987? As I wrestled with that question, I began to see his love
and concern for us. God kept it hidden because he wanted me
to marry Pat. She is a great woman and wife. My life would be
so impoverished without her, but I probably would have
missed that blessing had I known earlier. God wanted our
three sons to be born. Each is a blessing and a treasure, but we
would have missed that had we known earlier. God also knew

that we needed to be in a community of brothers and sisters in Christ at church and at the seminary who would love us and care for us at this darkest hour, so he withheld that information, not because he accidently overlooked giving it to us, nor because he is an uncaring, evil God who delights in seeing his children suffer. I have come to understand that he withheld it as a sign of his great care for us. There is never a good time to receive such news, but God knew that this was exactly the right time.

I have written at length about the need to show those who suffer that we care, because I am convinced this is so very crucial. We must show those who are hurting that we really do care, not only by saying it but also by showing it through our deeds. Above all, we must not avoid those who suffer. We must be there with them, even if only to listen. Your presence and willingness to listen and help say enough. They say you care. When we keep our distance from those who suffer, we confirm their worst fears that no one cares and no one will help. Show them that someone cares, not only when the initial shock comes, but in the weeks and months and years that follow. There is a sense in which one never completely recovers from tragedy. The need for the love and concern of others is always there.

Before I began my teaching ministry, I pastored a church for two years. My experiences in dealing with Pat's disease have impacted me greatly. If I were ever to pastor again, I know one thing I would definitely do. At the very outset, I would work with church leaders to identify all the people in the congregation with special needs. And I would see to it that at least once every week (and no less than once every two weeks) someone in the church would contact those people. It wouldn't always be the pastor, nor need it always be someone in a position of leadership who would do this. The main thing is that we check with these people to see how they are doing and to help meet their needs. Though it may seem like a small investment of time and energy to those who do help, it reaps immeasurable benefits in the lives of those helped. People with special needs may have no contact whatsoever with anyone for weeks at a time. Your love and care for them may be the only thing that brings any light into their life and dispels their loneliness, and it may be the only reason that they continue on in the faith. Do not overlook or bypass these people. Make your care for them an integral part of your church's ministry!

In the midst of our problems, I was vividly reminded about how difficult it is to go on with life without hope. I didn't really begin to feel much relief from my pain until I began to see some rays of hope. The fact that God and others cared was reason for hope, as was the realization that God would give grace for each new day. In addition, friends who knew about our situation and about this disease could point to specific reasons for hope. For one thing, research on this disease continues. With advances in genetic engineering in the area of gene therapy, there is legitimate reason for hope. It is possible that neither a cure nor even much help will come in time to aid my wife. Still there is reason for hope because the disease in her case developed at first very slowly. In recent years her condition has deteriorated more rapidly, but she could be further along than she is. It is possible as well that in the next few years the deterioration might move more slowly again. Thankfully, research continues on this disease. In recent years, geneticists have been able to figure out what the Huntington gene does to kill cells. Though they have not yet come up with a cure, at least they seem to have some ideas about how to combat this disease. That, of course, is good news for any of our children who may get this disease. The oldest will be twenty-eight this year, but none of them has yet shown any signs of the disease. Ten to fifteen years in medical science is a long time.

Are these false hopes? I think not. I believe it is crucial that people have a reason for hope. We must not offer false hope, but when there are real grounds for hope we should be quick to point those out. Some of my colleagues are especially sensitive to this need. When a newspaper or journal article appears which chronicles some advance in research on Pat's disease, no matter how small or insignificant the development, they make a point to show me the article. They realize that it is difficult to go on without hope, so they bring these things to my attention.

Something else that helped me was focusing on the fact that in spite of what has happened, God is good. One particular incident brought that vividly to my attention. A little over a year after we first received news of my wife's condition, I was being considered for tenure where I teach. In the tenure review interview, I was asked a question that really stopped me in my tracks. One of the members of the committee asked, "In light of what you've been through, can you still say that God is good?" Though I answered affirmatively, I did so somewhat hesitantly. I realized that I had been focusing so much on the problems and on what God *hadn't* done that I really hadn't paid enough attention to all the evidence of his goodness in my life.

In the months that followed, I thought a lot about how many things were going well for us. I believe that no matter how much pain and turmoil one suffers, it helps the sufferer to focus on the ways that God has shown his goodness. Even if a situation seems absolutely terrible, upon reflection one can probably imagine ways for it to be worse. Counting one's blessings may seem trite, but it does in fact give a different perspective on one's encroaching troubles.

In our case, there were many evidences of God's goodness. For one thing, in its early stages the disease had progressed very slowly in my wife's case. When doctors heard how long Pat has had symptoms, and when they saw where she was at the time, they found it hard to believe. Of course, in more recent years there has been significant deterioration, and there are no guarantees about the disease's future progression, but I can always be thankful for the extra years of relative normality in her condition that we had for a long time.

The love and concern shown to us by other Christians continue, and periodically I am again reminded of God's goodness as I hear of people literally all over the world who have heard about this and are praying for us. In addition, I have often thought that it is a blessing to live at this time in history! During early parts of the twentieth century (let alone earlier), little was known about Huntington's Chorea. Now it is known that there is a physiological base to this disease, not a psychological one. As research has advanced, within the last fifteen to twenty years the chromosome and the exact genetic marker involved in this disease have been identified. And, as already noted, scientists and physicians continue to work on combating and perhaps even curing the disease. My wife could have lived at any other time in history and still had this disease. That she and our children live now we take as another sign of God's special goodness to us.

Then, while this disease is a major challenge, many other things in our lives are going very well. The Lord has allowed Pat and me to travel extensively throughout the world to minister in churches and Bible schools. The ministry at Trinity continues to be a great joy, and God has blessed us in many other areas of our lives. When I look at these things, I can truly say that God has been and is good to us. It is easy to focus on what is going wrong. But when you realize that we live in a world where Satan is so dominant and sin so rampant, it is amazing that anything ever goes right! The fact that many things do go right is ample evidence of God's grace and goodness to us. Surely, we don't deserve it, and he isn't obligated to give it, but he does.

I am continually reminded of 1 Peter 5:7 (already mentioned in earlier chapters). That verse tells the reader to "cast all your anxiety on him, because he cares for you." Usually, we focus on the first part of that verse as we remind one another not to worry about what is happening. The latter part of the verse explains *why* we should do this, and I believe it is most instructive. Peter could have written, "Cast all your anxiety on him because he is powerful enough to do something about it." Or "because he knows the answer to your problems." Either of those thoughts would be just as true as what Peter wrote, but I'm glad Peter wrote what he did. It's as if he was saying, "Of course, he's powerful enough and intelligent enough to know and do something about our problems. He wouldn't be God if he weren't. What we want to know, though, is whether he cares enough to help us. And he does."

Indeed, God does care. Everywhere in our lives, in spite of what may be happening, we can find ample signs that God cares—if we only look for them. God cares because he is so good. Focusing on those truths, as well as reflecting on the many expressions of his goodness, won't entirely remove the pain and the doubts, but it can definitely help sufferers feel more comfortable with God.

CHAPTER 5

HIDING THE FUTURE

*I*n spite of all these encouragements in the midst of affliction, there was still the nagging question of how this could have happened to us. After all, it is not just that my wife is a Christian and has given her life in service to the Lord. The question of why this should happen to her is especially nagging, because it couldn't be God's retribution upon her for any sin she committed in her life. That she would get this disease was decided the moment she was conceived!

Be Angry at Sin

As I thought about that, I was reminded of an unpopular but very important biblical truth. It is that things like this happen because we live in a fallen world. God told Adam and Eve that if they disobeyed him, they would die (Gen. 2:17). They disobeyed, and the curse fell on them, and the apostle Paul reminds us that it fell on all of us as well (Rom. 5:12). Another way to say this is that Adam's sin and its consequences have been imputed or "credited" to the whole race. But if people die, they must die of something. There are many possible causes of death, and disease is one of them. When one realizes this, one understands that though my wife committed no specific sin after birth that brought this disease upon her, this has in fact happened because of her sin in Adam—though she is no more and no less responsible than the rest of us. Of course, that isn't the most comforting thought, but it is a sober reminder that this is our fault and not God's. And, God did warn us.

The main lesson to learn from this, however, is the enormity of sin and the need to hate it. Shortly after the news of Pat's disease came, I received what seemed to be a rather strange note of condolence from a friend who was teaching at another seminary. After expressing his sorrow over the news, he wrote, "I can just imagine how angry you must be right now at sin." Frankly, I thought that was a rather odd way to console someone. I knew that sin was the last target of my anger, if it was a focus at all.

And yet as I thought about my friend's note, I realized that he was absolutely right. These kinds of tragic events occur because we live in a fallen world. We may think our sins are a trifling matter. But when one hears the diagnosis of a terminal disease, or when one stands at the grave of a loved one, as we have at my mother's and father's graves within the last decade and a half, one has a vivid illustration of how terrible sin is. God said it would lead to this, but we don't take that warning as seriously as we should until something like this happens.

We may think of sin as trivial, but it isn't. We may also think the punishment of disease, troubles, and death far outweighs the crime of a little sin. That only underscores how far we are from God's perspective on these things. In light of our relative comfort with sin, a "little sin" doesn't seem so bad. From the perspective of an absolutely perfect God who has nothing to do with sin, it is atrocious.

Think of it in these terms. If you are a parent, you brought children into the world. When they arrived, they were totally helpless and depended on you for everything. You nurtured them and provided for their needs. You have loved them deeply, and you express that love in many different ways. In response, all you ask is that your children obey a few simple rules. How do you feel when they disobey? Doesn't it seem like the height of ingratitude to take so much from you and then refuse to follow a few rules? Surely, their disobedience seems far more serious to you than to them. How much more must it hurt God, who has given us so much and who moment by moment sustains us in existence, when we disobey him! Viewed from our perspective, sin isn't so bad, but viewing it from God's viewpoint, we should see that we need a different perspective on sin altogether.

My friend was right. If we see sin from God's perspective, we need to hate it. When we see where sin ultimately leads, we begin to understand how truly serious it is, and how much we ought to resist it. I can't say this will greatly comfort most of us, but it may help to focus our anger in the right direction. It may also help us to feel more comfortable with God as we realize that ultimately we have brought these things on ourselves. God warned us, but *we* wouldn't listen. Thank God that now in our troubles *he* will listen, forgive, and restore!

Helping Yourself by Helping Others

Other things also helped me cope with our situation. I mentioned earlier that I was having various physical problems and that the stress from my wife's news only made matters worse for me. Within a few months I was in great pain and was of little use to anyone. I didn't have the physical stamina to preach, nor the energy to make it through my classes. I not only felt that our situation was helpless and hopeless, but I also felt that I was useless and that I was adding to the problem by requiring attention that should have been placed elsewhere.

As with many people, my feelings of self-worth are tied in large part to my work and productivity. Being barely able to function made my sense of hopelessness worse.

In the midst of this dilemma, the Lord gave me opportunities to do things that helped other people. This was very helpful because it gave me a chance to get my focus off our problems and on someone else's needs. Even more, it showed me that I could still be useful. Gradually, as I regained strength and was able to do more, I became increasingly thankful that I could do anything, let alone help others who had shown us so much love and concern.

If you are wrestling with some affliction, as you are able, seek ways to help others. There is therapeutic value in getting your eyes off your problems and in seeing again that you can be of use to others. This helped somewhat to lift my burdens and showed me that when others, including my family, needed me, through God's enablement I would be able to help them.

Where Do We Go from Here?

After many months of grieving and some healing as a result of the things I have mentioned, I began to ask myself how I would ultimately respond to our problems. I began to consider my options. Would I continue to grieve and fall apart? I had already done that, and it solved nothing. With that approach, there had been little improvement in my own outlook, and I was of little help to anyone else. I concluded that this approach would in no way solve our problems. My wife still needed a husband, my children a father, and my students a teacher; for me to fall apart wouldn't help any of them. That option seemed a dead end. As Scripture says, there is a time to mourn (Eccl. 3:4), but then one must get on with one's life.

Another option was to get on with my life but exclude God from it. Many people choose this option in the face of affliction. They conclude either that there is no God, or they decide that there is but that they will fight him. Neither was acceptable for me. Though there was still some leftover anger toward God, I had seen too many evidences of his working in my life to doubt his existence. It made no sense to devote my life to propagating the view that God doesn't exist or that he is uninvolved with us. Even if that were true, there were surely more productive things I could do with my life.

Rejecting God's existence was totally unsatisfactory, but choosing to fight him was no better. God's goodness through-out my life—even now in this circumstance—didn't warrant my turning from him. Moreover, it is lunacy to pick a fight you can't win. In addition, it is beyond lunacy to fight someone who, rather than being the cause of your problems, is the only possible answer to them.

Another option was to take a Kierkegaardian leap of faith and trust that somehow this all made sense, though I could explain none of it. In other words, I could simply ignore and bypass the intellect and throw myself on God in the hope that he was there. Some might find that attractive, but it wasn't a live option for me. It is not my nature to sacrifice intellect so completely. The questions and the lack of peace would be there until my mind was settled. I didn't expect to find all the answers, but I knew I had to find many of them.

The only real option for me was clear—to continue trust-ing and worshipping God and to get on with my life. I had to stop the seemingly interminable, deep grieving and allow emotional healing to continue. I had to focus on answers that would satisfy the emotional dimensions of my struggle and would at the same time give enough intellectual answers to warrant peace of mind. I realized that I couldn't wait until all those answers arrived to continue with life, for too many people needed my help, and I needed to help them.

As I began to take this approach to my problems (and at some point we all must decide how to respond to our problems), I focused more on the positive things I've already mentioned. The healing and coping process continues to this day, as it will through the rest of my life. I still wrestle with these issues, and there is always great emotional pain as I see Pat's disease get worse. But God has allowed me to function again, and there is progress in dealing with these hurts.

I also came to see that there are few people who can totally control the circumstances in which they live and minister. Elijah couldn't, and neither could Jeremiah, Daniel, or the apostle Paul. When tragedy strikes, one must at some time face a crucial decision—*either* let the tragedy destroy you, and then you accomplish little of benefit for anyone, including yourself; *or* choose instead to live for God in spite of the circumstances. That is, "Play the hand life has dealt you," so to speak, and make the best out of a difficult situation. The apostle Paul is a great example of how to make the most out of bad situations. Put Paul in prison on one occasion, and he converts the jailer to Christ. Put him in prison on another occasion and he writes beautiful letters to growing churches (Ephesians, Philippians, Colossians, Philemon), letters that become part of Holy Writ! In a similar way, for me the second option is the only reasonable choice, and it entails that I keep on trusting God in spite of what is happening.

Hiding the Future So We'll Trust Him

God is not only there when the shock of tragic news first comes. At various points along the way when we are ready to hear it, he adds a further word of comfort, encouragement, and enlightenment. One of those words of help comes from what might seem a rather strange source of comfort, a passage in Ecclesiastes. The passage is Ecclesiastes 7:13–14, and the thrust of it is that God hides the future from us so that we will trust him. The passage reads:

> Consider what God has done: Who can straighten what he has made crooked? When times are good, be happy; but when times are bad, consider: God has made the one as well as the other. Therefore, a man cannot discover anything about his future.

The context of these verses is significant. The sixth and seventh chapters of Ecclesiastes contain a series of aphorisms or dictums, though it isn't always easy to see how they fit together. Much of chapter 7 focuses on things that at first appear undesirable in order to show that they do in fact have a certain benefit. The previous chapter shows that things which look good also have a downside. The ultimate message is that we can't always take things at face value, nor should we think we can always understand them. If this is true of things we do and experience, how much more is it true of God and his ways!

In verses 13–14 especially, the author of Ecclesiastes emphasizes the sovereign power of God. Some think the rhetorical question, "Who can straighten what he has made crooked?" means that if God brings something we consider evil, we can't make it good (straighten it). Put another way, we can't overturn God's powerful hand. While this interpretation surely fits verse 14 and its teaching about God's bringing of adversity, I think the writer's point is even more general. That is, just as no one can straighten what God bends, no one can bend what he straightens. No one can overturn what God does, regardless of what it is; man must simply submit to God's providence.

All of this suggests that adversity and prosperity are alike under God's hand. Indeed, the Teacher of Ecclesiastes confirms that in verse 14. God sends both good and bad. He tells us to be happy in the good days. That may seem strange, since most people are inclined to be happy in times of prosperity. However, the injunction to be happy makes an abundant amount of sense. Some people will allow themselves only so much prosperity before they begin to worry about the future. It's as though they are keeping score of how many good things are happening, because they believe that we can only have just so much "good luck" before we are due for some really "bad luck." It's as if they think that the more things go well, the more they are storing up and postponing some major calamities. Rather than enjoying their present blessings, they worry about how badly they are going to get clobbered once the good times run out. Of course, no one really knows what will come next, so all this worrying about future evil coming our way accomplishes nothing. Just as it is true that things which start out bad can wind up being good, and vice versa, it is also true that when times are good for us, there may be more good times on the docket. But even if what's up next on the agenda of our lives is suffering, why lose the enjoyment of the present? So, the Teacher tells us to be happy. Don't let the evil that may be just around the corner destroy the happiness of the present!

The writer then says that in evil days, we should "consider." He doesn't say that in evil days we should be sad. He doesn't need to, because that comes naturally. Instead, we should consider. What should we consider or think about?

We should think about what has happened, think about the alternation of good and bad, and realize that no one knows when either will come. In fact, what appears to be good may turn out evil, and vice versa. Things aren't always what they seem. But what we should most consider is that God has made both good and bad times, and that he pieces them together in our lives in such a way that we won't know what will happen in the future.

Is this really what the passage says? Indeed it is, for the writer says that God puts together the events of our lives in such a way that "a man cannot discover anything about his future"; that is, God structures our personal histories in a way that conceals the future. Why does God hide the future from us? I wrestled with that question, and there was only one answer that made sense (though it isn't stated in the text). If we don't know what will happen in the future, our only option is to wait on the Lord to reveal what will come next and to trust him about our future. We may want to change what God will do, but verse 13 reminds us that we can't. We must submit to his providences and simply trust him. If we knew the details of our future, we might think we could manipulate and control it as we want without relying on God at all. In short, we might think there was no need to trust God.

God conceals the future, then, so that we must trust him. You can see how this truth fits my family's situation so well. It wasn't only relevant before we learned the news that was for so long available but unknown to us; it is relevant now as we contemplate the course of this disease and the future of each of our children.

As I thought about this truth, however, I was again troubled. If God conceals the future so that we must trust him, does that mean God manipulates people and events so that we will love and trust him? Is it possible that he can't get our trust any other way, so he manipulates things to force us to trust him? If that is so, this is no God worthy of praise and worship! Nor is he a good God! This is a conniving, manipulative God who has created us solely for his benefit and really doesn't care about us after all.

Upon further reflection, however, I realized that God isn't an evil God at all. By concealing the future, God does make us trust him, but this is compassion, not manipulation! It is compassionate in a number of ways.

Knowing the details of our future would very probably be harmful to us. Suppose our future would be good. No doubt we would be relieved, but the joy of discovery would be gone. What should be great when it happens would lose its excitement as a surprise. We might even be bored, and the joy of anticipation would be gone. Suppose one Christmas when you were a child you knew exactly what you were getting for Christmas, even though your parents thought you didn't know. Wouldn't that somewhat spoil your joy of discovery on Christmas eve or morning when you open your presents? Isn't part of the fun of Christmas that until presents are opened, anything seems possible—we can imagine any number of delightful gifts waiting for us? But if we already know what we're getting, the joy of anticipating something new and unknown is largely removed. Not only that, but if Mom and Dad think you don't know what you're getting, you have to act surprised when you see your presents, even if you've known for a long time what they are. Some of us just aren't good enough actors to pull off that one!

Revealing a good future might also make us complacent in our relation to God, and that would be bad. Since the future will be good, we might conclude that we don't need to rely on

God, but obviously we do. And if the future is good and we know it, we might easily become inattentive to the present and impatient to get to the future as we eagerly await it. This sometimes happens to us even without knowing the specifics of the future. When we anticipate an exciting vacation, we become impatient with the present. In essence, we overlook the good things that are happening now and lose the present. That is unfortunate, for God may have significant work for us to do now and great blessings in the present as well.

On the other hand, suppose our future is evil. Unless the Lord returns first for his Church, Scripture and common sense teach that the ultimate end of this life for us all will be death, and death is evil. If we knew in advance the circumstances of our death, or if we knew what evils would befall us along the way, we might be totally horrified and unable to act as fear paralyzed us. Hiding the future is compassionate, because knowing the future might terrify us.

Hiding an evil future is also compassionate, because we must not ignore the present, but we might do that if we knew the future. We might spend much of our time worrying about the future or grieving over our anticipated misfortune. Even more, we might think that we could somehow change the future to avoid the foreknown evils. Of course, that is impossible, for as the Teacher says, no one can change what God has decided will happen. Why waste the present trying to change something you can't change? If we foolishly waste the present, at the end of life we will look back on our life with regrets over never really having lived at all.

As already mentioned, one of the things that our experiences have done for me is to focus my attention on the present. I don't want to know any more about the distant future than I have to. In fact, I am better able to cope when I focus on where my wife is today, rather than on where she may be in her condition somewhere down the road. We must not become so overly occupied with the future that we lose today. God has hidden the future, so we might trust him. He is compassionate in doing so.

God's hiding my family's future is compassionate, because we couldn't handle some of the information about the future if we had it. On November 4, 1987, I caught a glimpse of the future that just about destroyed me. I am more than willing now to take the future one day at a time. In most cases God compassionately reveals the details of our futures moment by moment, and that is enough. As Scripture says, "Each day has enough trouble of its own" (Matt. 6:34). I don't have tomorrow's grace yet, so I don't need to know tomorrow's evil today either!

CHAPTER 6

GRACE, JUSTICE, AND THE SUFFERING OF THE RIGHTEOUS

A ll of these things were sources of comfort and encouragement. Yet something was still wrong. There seemed to be a basic unfairness about our situation. Put simply, why was this happening to us, and not also to other people? Wasn't it unjust of God to ask us to bear this burden, especially when others have trials that are so much less catastrophic? I believe this is a sticking point for many people that makes it very difficult for them to live with God.

Please do not misunderstand this. I wouldn't wish our pain on anyone, but it seems only fair that if others escape, we should too. If God could keep others from this fate, why couldn't he keep us from it? Of course, he owes nothing to any of us per se, but justice seems to demand that we get at least as good a shake as the next family.

I suspect that most people who experience significant tragedy in their lives have thought this way at some point. I surely had those thoughts, but I came to see that they contain an error. When philosophers discuss the concept of justice, they distinguish between what is called *distributive justice* and *egalitarian justice*. With distributive justice, each person gets exactly what is deserved. If you do good, in strict justice you are owed good. If you do evil, in strict justice you deserve punishment. Egalitarian justice, however, gives everyone the same thing, regardless of merit or desert.

Now I saw the source of the problem. It isn't just that sufferers think distributive justice mandates a better fate for them (since they think they have done good). The complaint is that God should operate with egalitarian justice in his handling of the world. We expect him to treat everyone the same, and that means we should escape a specific affliction if others do! Otherwise, it seems that God has been unfair.

Once I remembered the distinction between these two types of justice, I immediately asked why God is obligated to dole out suffering and blessing on the basis of egalitarian justice. Given the demands of distributive justice, all sinners *deserve* nothing but punishment. Why, then, is God obligated to respond to us in egalitarian terms? I couldn't answer that. If God really did handle us according to egalitarian justice, we would all either experience the same torture or be equally blessed. But those ideas don't match the God described in Scripture. It was a tremendous help to realize that part of my anger stemmed from thinking that God is obligated to handle us with egalitarian justice, even though he isn't. Once I realized that he has no such obligation, I understood that much of my anger rested on a misunderstanding of what God should be expected to do.

Now this didn't completely solve the problem. Even if God isn't obligated to give any of us more than we deserve, and even if we deserve punishment for our sin, still God has chosen to be *gracious* to some. If you are suffering from some affliction, you may feel that God should extend the same grace to you as he has to those who never confront your affliction. God must be unjust, then, for not extending as much grace to you as to the next person.

This objection is very understandable, and I believe it was at the heart of what was then bothering me. Nonetheless, it is still wrong. The objection now has escalated from a demand that God treat us with egalitarian *justice* to a demand that God grant us egalitarian *grace*.

In two respects this demand is wrong. In the first place, God is no more obligated to give the same grace to everyone than he is to give egalitarian justice to all. He is only obligated to distribute what we deserve. The other point is that since we are talking about granting grace, the charge that God has been *unjust* because he gave someone else more *grace* (and this is really what the sufferer is complaining about) is totally misguided.

Grace is unmerited favor, meaning that you get something good that you don't deserve and didn't earn. If neither my neighbor nor I merit grace at all (if we deserved it, it wouldn't be grace, but justice) it can't be *unjust* that my neighbor gets more grace than I. It can only be unjust if God is obligated to treat us with egalitarian grace, and he surely isn't. In fact, he isn't *obligated* to treat us with any kind of grace. Grace precludes obligation! That's why it's grace and not justice. Hence, it can't be unjust if someone gets more grace than another. If God graciously chooses to give some of us a better (by our evaluation) lot than others, he has done nothing wrong. We have no right to place requirements on how and when God distributes grace; if we did, that would turn it into justice.

This distinction between grace and justice is crucial. Many people think that grace is the opposite of injustice. Hence, when God doesn't give them grace, they conclude that God has treated them unfairly. But the opposite of injustice is justice; grace is an entirely different thing! Thus, grace is neither fair nor unfair, because fairness and unfairness invoke the concept of justice. Grace has nothing to do with justice; it's a different commodity altogether.

One of Jesus' parables illustrates the point very vividly. It is the parable of the landowner and the workers in his vineyard, recorded in Matthew 20:1–16. In many respects this is a strange and difficult parable, but its message about the relation of grace to justice is extremely important! It teaches that God has the right to give grace as he chooses, and when he does, no one has the right to envy those who receive God's unmerited favor or to complain that God treated him or her unfairly because he didn't grant them grace.

The parable begins with Jesus saying that this parable illustrates how he handles things in the kingdom of heaven (v. 1). Jesus says that a landowner went out early in the morning to hire workers for his vineyard. In order to understand the story more fully, it is important to know that the Jews divided the day from sunrise to sunset into twelve parts. Thus, the sixth hour would be noon, the third would be 9 a.m., the ninth hour would be 3 p.m., and the eleventh hour would be 5 p.m., just a little while before quitting time. The landowner agreed to pay those hired first in the day a denarius for a whole day of work, and he sent them off to work (v. 2). In fact, it is only with these first workers that he makes a promise of a specific amount of money for their work. According to verses 3–5, he hired more workers at 9 a.m., noon, and 3 p.m. (the third, sixth, and ninth hours). In each instance, he told them to go into the vineyard and work, and he promised that he would give them whatever is right. He didn't say how much money would be right, but in essence, he promised to do what was fair.

About an hour before quitting time, he saw some other workers who hadn't worked during the day. He sent them out to
work and told them that he would give them whatever is right
(vv. 6–7). Only in the case of the workers hired first did the
landowner agree on a specific wage. All the remaining workers by going to work agreed to trust that the landowner would
do right by them.

At the end of the day, the landowner told his steward to
call in all the workers and pay them. He stipulated, however,
that the steward should first pay those hired last and work his
way back to those hired first. Since Jesus crafted the parable in
this way, we get to hear the response of the workers hired first,
and only after giving their response could Jesus make the point
of his parable.

What would he pay those hired later in the day? Justice
would seem to dictate that he pay them less than what he paid
those hired early in the day. But he didn't. He paid the workers hired last a denarius. In fact, it seems that he gave each of
the laborers a denarius (v. 9). When those hired first saw that
those hired last received a denarius, they must have been
"licking their chops," expecting a bonanza. They thought,
*After all, if those who did next to nothing get a denarius, those who
have worked the whole day should get more.* But the steward paid
to each of those hired first in the day the exact same amount
he paid to everyone else, a denarius (v. 10).

The workers hired first were furious! They had done most
of the work. They had labored through the heat of the day, and
yet they received no more pay than those hired just about an
hour before quitting time. That seemed totally unfair to them,
and they complained to the landowner about what he had
done. Surely they should have received more than these other
workers!

What these workers did is typical of human nature. Somebody got a better deal in life than I did, and that's not fair. We can't stand it when others prosper and we don't, especially if we think we are just as good as they are or that we have worked just as hard or harder than they. We complain that if there were any justice is the world, we would succeed and be blessed at least as much as others.

In verses 13–15 we find the landowner's answer. The landowner replied that he had done nothing wrong in his treatment of them. Didn't he agree to pay them a denarius for a day's work? Of course, he did (v. 2). They did the work, and he paid them. Justice says that you pay exactly what you owe. The landowner made a deal with the workers. They kept their part of the bargain, and so did he. He gave them exactly what he promised; they had no reason for such anger, for he had treated them fairly.

In verse 15 we read that the landowner then asked them a crucial question: Didn't he have a right to do whatever he wanted with his money? If he wanted to pay those hired later in the day exactly what he paid those hired first, didn't he have a right to do that? Is the problem here that the workers hired first are envious of those who seemed to get a better deal than they did (v. 15)? Indeed, it is. The landowner had been generous (gracious) to these other workers, and the workers hired first were in effect demanding that the landowner treat everyone with justice—that is, he gave each exactly what he had earned, merited, deserved. Nothing less and certainly nothing more.

But think again about the promise the landowner made to all the laborers except the first hired. He told them that he would give them whatever was right, but he never stipulated a specific monetary amount. His only obligation was to do something right (just) for them. Was giving them each a denarius a case of being just or right to them? Yes and no. Yes, because if those who worked less than the whole day received the same as those hired first in the day, the landowner certainly hadn't been unjust to those who worked a shorter time. He had certainly done for them what anyone should call right.

On the other hand, he wasn't just to those hired later in the day, but not because he was unjust to them! As it turned out, he decided to be more than just—he decided to be gracious. Had he done something wrong? Of course not. Whatever was owed, he paid, but out of the goodness of his heart in some cases he gave well beyond anything that was owed. It is all right not to give exactly what is owed as long as you don't give *less* than is owed. In this case, the landowner gave more. That's not justice or injustice! It's grace! But what's so wrong with giving some people exactly what they deserve (justice) while granting to others more than they deserve (grace)? After all, didn't the landowner have a right to do with his money what he wanted? Whose money (whose grace) is it, anyway?!

So, then, the landowner was fair (just) to those hired first, because he gave them exactly what he had promised and what they had earned. But still, isn't there a sense in which the landowner still *owed* them more, since he gave the workers hired later more than they deserved? No, he did not, and this is the crucial point! He didn't owe them more, because *grace is never owed!* That's why it's grace and not justice, a totally different thing. The workers hired first in the day were envious of the grace given to the other workers. Jesus' point was that they had no reason to be angry at the landowner or to envy their coworkers. How small of them to begrudge these others the grace they received, and to think the landowner was unfair because he *owed* them more. Grace is never *owed* to anyone, so God cannot justly be accused of failing to do something he should have done when someone else receives grace that we didn't get.

Jesus ends this parable by affirming it shows that the last shall be first and the first shall be last. What did Jesus mean? We must understand this within the context of the discussion between Jesus and his disciples, recorded at the end of chapter 9 (vv. 16–30). Jesus has just told the rich young man the cost of discipleship. It involves selling his earthly possession, giving to the poor, and then following Christ. The disciples were very much disturbed by this saying. Peter tells the Lord that he and the others have left everything to follow Christ; what will God do for them? Jesus replies that those who leave earthly possessions and family will be given a position of prominence in the kingdom when Christ reigns. They can't sacrifice more than God will bless them. However, Jesus reminds them that many who are last will be first, and the first will be last.

Amid this context, Jesus then tells the parable of the landowner and the laborers in his vineyard. At its end (Matt. 20:16), Jesus repeats the point that the last will be first and the first will be last. This sounds strange, but within the context of the parable, I believe it makes an abundant amount of sense. If our position in the kingdom were based on things like our earthly possessions, fame, and accomplishments, then those with the most impressive résumés would have the greatest authority in the kingdom. On the other hand, if God bases privilege and position in the kingdom on the magnanimity of his grace, then our accomplishments aren't so important, and even someone who in this life was socially and economically last could be placed in a position of prominence. If a loving heavenly Father wants to extend them such grace, the rest of us have no right to be offended or complain!

I believe that these great truths apply to my situation and to every instance where someone feels that God has treated them unfairly because they don't receive exemption from problems that others escape. God isn't obligated to keep me from my trials just because he hasn't given you those afflictions. Giving grace to you doesn't mean he has been unfair to me. He never obligated himself to give me such grace, so there is no injustice in what he has done (or not done). I have no right to think he has been unjust or unfair, for grace is never owed. I have no right to envy you when God has given you a grace he has withheld from me, for he has a right to do with his own grace what he chooses.

Rather than envying the grace given to others, I should be thankful that they have received grace. Surely I would not be happy to see God withhold grace so that others are struck with the same tragedy that has befallen us! Moreover, we must all be careful not to assume that because God has withheld *this* grace from us that he has withheld *all* grace. There are too many examples in my life of God's unmerited favor to think that. Not least among those undeserved blessings are the wonderful wife and children he has given me!

These principles about justice and grace won't likely relieve the pain of suffering, but they can help dissipate anger toward God. I have found them to be liberating, and I frequently remind myself of these principles when I am inclined to lament that God has given others an apparently easier lot than mine.

There is another way that we can relate to grace. Suppose that you are the one receiving God's gracious exemption from suffering. Don't reject those who suffer as morally and spiritually inferior to you just because you received grace! You didn't get that grace because you are better—if you had, it would have come to you as a reward for your accomplishments. But that's not grace, that's justice! No one should feel superior for having received grace, for they didn't do something to earn it—that's why it's grace!

Since you don't get grace because you deserve it, when others don't get the same grace you do, should you feel guilty that they got affliction while you received grace? These questions are even relevant to my family's situation. Earlier I mentioned the dilemma about whether to have our children tested for Huntington's Disease. There are obvious potential problems for those found to carry the gene. But there are also possible difficulties for those who know they won't get the disease. For example, it isn't uncommon for those who find that they won't get the disease to feel guilty that they will escape while their brothers or sisters won't.

Viewed in the light of what I have been saying, I believe that no one should feel guilty for escaping affliction. If what happens were totally a matter of justice—that is, if we all were given exactly what we deserve—then I should feel guilty if you suffer and I don't. But this isn't a matter of simple justice. It is a matter of grace. If God in his sovereign wisdom chooses to give you grace, don't feel guilty as though either you or God has done something wrong. Rather, rejoice and praise him for the grace that spared you the suffering. In addition, feel compassion toward those who haven't escaped, and do whatever you can to help them bear their burdens!

If you are the recipient of affliction, never begrudge the grace God gives to others. If you receive God's gracious exemption from suffering, praise him and show compassion to those who suffer. Don't apologize for receiving grace, and don't seek further affliction in order to "even things out" between you and those who are suffering. Affliction will find its way to your doorstep soon enough. Praise God for the grace!

These principles about grace and justice also apply to many other areas of our lives. Let me mention two that relate to salvation. Sometimes critics of Christianity complain that our God is said to have power to save anyone from sin that he wants. In fact, he could save us all, if he wanted. But Calvinist Christians then add that he has chosen only to save some; the rest are left for eternal damnation. How can it be fair to save only some when, as Christians claim, no one merits salvation?

You don't have to believe in divine election to know that God doesn't save everyone. But are the critics right; has God been unfair in his handling of salvation? If we are asking that God handle the granting of salvation with fairness, then we are invoking the concept of justice. But if justice is required, then all of us are in deep trouble. Scripture and common sense tell us that all have sinned and are guilty before God. If God were to treat us in strict justice, no one would be saved. However, a gracious God has decided to save some people for a life of eternal fellowship with him and abundant life now; none of those saved merits salvation. Some complain that others are no more nor less deserving, but they aren't saved. This is true, but if we demand that God treat us with justice, then those not saved receive their just due. To complain that God owes these people salvation since he has graciously granted it to others is to place obligations on grace. But grace cannot be obligated; it is a free gift bestowed out of the generous heart of the giver. Those who don't get saving grace have nothing to complain about, for God hasn't failed to do something for them that he owed!

These principles about the relation of grace to justice also apply to another item relating to God's handling of salvation. Some of us decided early in life to give up much of what the world counts as pleasure in order to trust Christ as Savior and live for him. We did so, not because we wouldn't have enjoyed any of these pleasures, but because we were informed that Christians just don't do such things. On the other hand, others accept Christ late in life, some even while in the throes of a terminal disease. Some may have turned to Christ only after having indulged in all of the pleasures and even evils this world has to offer. Think of the thief crucified next to Christ. As he was dying, he placed his faith and trust in Christ. Christ told him that he would be with Christ in paradise that very same day.

Readers who have known Christ as personal Savior for much of your life, I have a question for you. When you get to heaven, are you going to say something like the following to the Lord? "Lord, I'm just so thrilled to be here! Thank you so much for saving me! But, Lord there is something that troubles me. That repentant thief who was crucified next to you—I don't know what he did in his life, but at least he did something bad enough to get himself crucified. On the other hand, I followed you most of my life. There are many things I would have enjoyed doing, but I didn't so that I could faithfully follow you. Are you going to tell me, Lord, that I am no more saved than that repentant thief who turned to you only in the last minutes of his life? That's not fair, Lord! For at least the first five hundred thousand years of eternity you should leave him outside the walls of heaven (no, don't cast him into hell; after all, he did trust you as Savior)! And then when you do bring him inside heaven's gates, don't give him one of those bright shiny mansions on Main Street. Put him far from sight—a back alley or even someone's garage would be appropriate for him!"

When you get to heaven, are you going to say that to the Lord? Of course not! You won't be unhappy that others received eternal life after a life of indulgence in sin, while you chose to live a life of obedience to God. Would you prefer that God not extend them grace so that they would spend eternity separated from God—just because they trusted Christ late in life? Of course not. Never begrudge someone the grace God gives them! I am delighted that our God is so gracious and patient with sinners that he leaves the door to salvation open even for those who repeatedly reject him before they turn to him as Savior. There is no room for envying the grace God gives to others!

Even those who don't know Christ as Savior have still received grace from his hand. Otherwise, they would have received judgment long ago, as would those who know Christ. And even though my family and I didn't receive grace that exempts us from Huntington's Disease, we are still the recipients of his grace in many areas of our life. These truths about grace and justice don't make what has happened good, but understanding them did remove a huge obstacle to fellowship between the Lord and me. He hasn't failed to give me grace he owed, but he has granted many gracious blessings to me and my family that he also didn't owe. Grace is not fair, but it isn't unfair either! It's something entirely different, and I thank God for it!

CHAPTER 7

USING AFFLICTION FOR OUR GOOD

I have shared something of my own struggles with the religious problem of evil and some of the things that have helped me cope with our family situation. The religious problem isn't primarily an intellectual struggle, but rather an emotional one. That doesn't mean, however, there are no intellectual dimensions to it, for of course what one thinks affects how one feels.

There is another line of intellectual answers that can help in ministering to the hurting. I am thinking of the uses of affliction. Though God isn't the author of evil and affliction, he does allow these things to happen. When they do, God is not helpless to use them to accomplish positive things in our lives. While the affliction isn't good, it can serve as an occasion for God to bring some good out of what is evil. The fact that God does this and that we can see him working in our lives can reassure us that his hand is still upon us. He isn't angry at us, and we aren't abandoned. Realizing that God didn't bring this affliction but is doing something positive and for our benefit in the midst of it can help us realize that the Creator is good and that he is worthy of our worship.

I want to present a series of things God can do in the life of the afflicted. I have found these principles encouraging, though they weren't particularly helpful in the earlier stages of my own struggles. When someone is still reeling from the shock of tragedy, it won't likely help to say, "Take heart, there are many positive things God can do through this affliction, and I want to share them with you." At that point, the sufferer is too hurt, too angry, and too much in shock to grasp fully the import of this kind of approach. If you begin to rehearse the beneficial uses of suffering, the afflicted may quickly inform you that they would gladly forgo any of these positive things since they must come through affliction. Or, the sufferer may simply ask why, if God can bring good out of evil, he can't bring good out of good.

It is wisest, then, to allow the sufferer time to begin healing. Share the things I mentioned in previous chapters, as opportunities arise. At some point in the healing process, the sufferer will be ready to hear the things that follow.

First, let me be clear about what the following information does not mean. Pointing to the uses of suffering may appear at first blush to be saying that these positive outcomes are the reasons God allows suffering in the first place. It may even appear that I am saying these uses of suffering prove that God is a good God in spite of the evil in our world.

That is not what I am saying, for I don't believe it to be the case. If that's what I was saying, I would be holding God to be a good God despite the fact that he hasn't removed suffering and evil because he is able to use evil as a means to accomplish a good end. But to say that is to say the end justifies the means. I don't hold that view of right and wrong, and I don't believe Scripture teaches such an ethic.

The information I'll share in this and the next two chapters is not meant to *justify* God's ways to mankind, the sort of thing Christian philosophers and theologians do when they tackle intellectual questions about why an all-loving, all-powerful God would allow evil in our world. I have addressed such questions elsewhere at length.[1]

There is a difference, however, between justifying God as good in spite of evil and helping the afflicted feel more positive toward God in spite of their affliction. Many things can help remove emotional and spiritual pain as the afflicted seek to live at peace with the God who has allowed this pain. What I offer now is help for healing the breach in the sufferer's relation to God.

How, then, might God use affliction in the life of the righteous sufferer?[2] There are many ways, and I have divided them into ten basic categories. It is natural to think that in any given instance of suffering, God is using it to accomplish only one thing. If we don't immediately sense what that is, frustration arises. However, in any actual case God may intend to accomplish a whole series of things rather than just one, and not just in the life of the sufferer alone. God may intend to accomplish something in the sufferer's life, something in the lives of those who know the sufferer, and something in regard to angelic and demonic forces. A particular case of suffering may have several uses of affliction at work.

What possible good might God accomplish in our lives through the afflictions we undergo? First, God may allow affliction for the same reason he had in the case recorded in John 9:1–3. In that situation, affliction provided an opportunity for God to manifest his power. In John 9, the disciples asked Jesus about a man blind from birth: "Who sinned, this man or his parents, that he was born blind?" Jesus rejected the common belief that all suffering must be a punishment for some specific sin. He answered instead, "Neither this man nor his parents sinned; but this happened so that the work of God might be displayed in his life." To the amazement of those who saw it, Christ then performed a miracle to restore the man's sight. Similarly, God sometimes allows affliction in the life of the righteous as a basis for some future work that demonstrates his power and glory.

During earlier years of Pat's dealing with Huntington's, we saw this happen to some extent. Though she showed some signs of the disease, doctors repeatedly mentioned how wonderful it was that the disease had progressed so slowly for so long. On more than one occasion we used those comments as an opportunity to state our belief that we weren't just lucky. Rather, this was evidence of the hand of God in her life. Even though deterioration has been more rapid in recent years, that can't negate the display of God's power in Pat's case in the early stages of this disease.

Second, God may use affliction to remove a cause for boasting. When things go smoothly in life, we tend to feel self-sufficient. Affliction reminds us that we aren't, and that we must ultimately rely on God. A classic illustration of this principle comes from the life of the apostle Paul. Paul had a thorn in the flesh, some sort of physical ailment whose exact nature Bible commentators debate. In 2 Corinthians 12:7, Paul says he pleaded with God to remove the thorn, but he didn't. Paul then wrote that if God had removed the problem, he might have thought too highly of himself in view of the significant revelations God had given to him. His thorn in the flesh was a constant reminder that there is no room for boasting. Sometimes God uses affliction similarly in our lives.

In the first two chapters of Job, we see a third way God uses the suffering of the righteous. God allowed Job's afflictions at least in part to demonstrate genuine faith to Satan. Satan claimed that the only reason Job served God was that it was worth Job's while. If God removed his hand of blessing from Job, Job would no longer serve him. God answered that Job served him out of genuine love, and he decided to prove that to Satan. Through Job's afflictions and through his faithfulness to God, Satan saw that there are those who actually do serve God out of true love, not because "it pays to do so."

God may use affliction in our life to accomplish some purpose *for us*, and at the same time use our response to show Satan and his legions that there are still those who love and serve God regardless of their personal circumstances in life. Others will see this as well. This is extremely important, for as Christians we claim to have the ultimate answers to life's problems. Of course, it is relatively easy to be a Christian when everything is going well. What many non-Christians want to know, however, is whether Christianity works when things go wrong. That's one of the true tests of any religion. If we turn from God in the midst of affliction, we communicate to those watching that at times of stress Christianity offers no more of an answer than any other religion or ideology. God still needs people today who will show others that even when life brings the unexpected and the tragic, they will continue to love and serve God, not because it pays to do so, but because he is worthy of devotion.

This is why Peter tells us that in the midst of affliction we must be ready to explain why we continue to hold on to our hope in God (1 Pet. 3:15). This verse is frequently taken out of context to show that Christians should always defend the faith in general. That is, the academic discipline of apologetics should be encouraged. However, that is neither the point nor the context of the verse. Peter is discussing the suffering of the righteous. He says that when suffering comes, and when we are challenged to explain why we continue to trust God and remain faithful to him in spite of what has happened, we must be ready to defend our continued hope. Our hope is that there is a God who knows what we are experiencing and cares. It is a hope that God will right the wrong that others do to afflict us. And it is a hope that God will deliver us from the pain and suffering we are enduring and that he will grant us his sustaining grace until he does remove the trial! Peter adds that our response must be both verbal and nonverbal (1 Pet. 3:15–17). That is, we must not only explain why we have hope and why Christianity makes a difference, but we must live as people for whom Christianity makes a real difference. We dare not use our affliction as an excuse to justify deserting Christian principles and disobeying God's Word.

Fourth, sometimes God uses affliction as an opportunity to demonstrate to believers and nonbelievers the concept of the body of Christ. According to 1 Corinthians 12:12–26, each believer in Christ as Savior is a member of the body of Christ. As Christians, we are related to one another through Christ, and we need one another. Moreover, verse 26 says, "If one part suffers, every part suffers with it." That means that when one suffers, all suffer, and when one rejoices, all rejoice. This is the ideal, but it doesn't always match our experience. Too often Christians treat one another as if there were total isolation among members of the body of Christ. To correct this mistaken attitude, God may on occasion use the affliction of one member of the body to show other members that believers need one another and must help one another.

Through affliction the body of Christ concept may be demonstrated in several different ways. Suffering gives opportunity for afflicted people to experience the compassionate love of God through other believers. It allows sufferers to understand experientially what it means to have their burdens carried (Gal. 6:2). As mentioned in previous chapters, these truths have been vividly reinforced to us on many occasions through the words and deeds of other believers who care.

In addition, suffering gives other believers the opportunity to express Christian love to those in need. When we help afflicted members of the body, we understand more fully how deeply we need one another. We experience as well what it means to show Christian love and compassion. In order to give us that opportunity to minister, God may allow affliction to strike another member of our spiritual family.

Jesus said that people would know that believers are his disciples if we love one another. Helping a suffering brother or sister is a tangible way to show that we are followers of Christ.

These are only some of the uses of suffering, for there are others. In the next chapter, I want to examine the relationship between suffering and personal holiness. As we shall see, there are many ways that God can use suffering to help us turn from sin and become more like Christ.

CHAPTER 8

SUFFERING AND HOLINESS

Scripture teaches that in a number of ways affliction in the life of the righteous promotes holiness. First Peter 4:1–2 makes the general point that the experience of suffering helps the believer to put away sin. Peter writes:

> Therefore, since Christ suffered in his body, arm yourselves also with the same attitude, because he who has suffered in his body is done with sin. As a result, he does not live the rest of his earthly life for evil human desires, but for the will of God.

When Peter says the sufferer "is done with sin," he is not saying that by suffering the believer is completely removed from the power, influence, or guilt of sin. As 1 John 1:8 teaches, "If we claim to be without sin, we deceive ourselves and the truth is not in us." It is impossible to remove sin's influence completely in this life. Instead, Peter means that afflictions have a way of driving believers away from committing specific acts of sin. They do so by helping us resist the temptations that surround us rather than yielding to them.

I have found this to be true in my own experience. In light of my family's situation, certain things that enticed me before pale in significance to the ultimate issues of life and death.

That is not to say that those things never tempt me or that I never sin. Rather, what has happened to my wife and family has helped tremendously to put those temptations in proper perspective. Life isn't about such enticements; much more important things are at stake. When affliction drives us from committing specific acts of sin, we draw closer to the Lord and view things more with the significance that he puts on them. This is evidence of the Holy Spirit at work in us to help us grow in holiness and conformity to the character of Jesus Christ.

Another way affliction promotes sanctification is by refining one's faith. First Peter 1:6–7 says,

In this you greatly rejoice, though now for a little while you may have had to suffer grief in all kinds of trials. These have come so that your faith—of greater worth than gold, which perishes even though refined by fire—may be proved genuine and may result in praise, glory and honor when Jesus Christ is revealed.

The focus of this test of faith isn't the test itself, but the outcome of the test. That is, the focus is the residue of faith that remains when the test is over. Peter's point isn't that the test itself is precious, for the test is suffering, and that is not more precious than gold. Rather, the faith left after the test is precious. Therefore, as Peter says, believers can rejoice in the midst of affliction because through these experiences God is refining their faith. The ultimate result is that at Christ's appearing the believer's tested faith will be found genuine and will result in praise and honor and glory.

Holiness is also promoted by suffering, when God uses it to educate believers in ways that cause them to grow closer to the Lord and to be more Christlike. For example, James 1:3–4,

Romans 5:3–4, and 1 Peter 5:10 teach that God develops in us perseverance or endurance through adversity. Hebrews 5:8 indicates that even Christ in his humanity learned obedience through suffering. Now, if God is to teach us anything, he must have our attention. When there is no affliction in our lives, it is easy to become overly self-sufficient and inattentive to what the Lord wants to teach as he desires to draw us closer to himself. When affliction comes, though we may be inclined to rebel against God, if we pay attention to what God is trying to teach us, we may instead learn things we might not have been otherwise open to hear.

Through difficult experiences believers can also draw closer to the Lord by catching a glimpse of his sovereignty and majesty such as they have never seen before. Job 42:2–4 records the response of a man who suffered as much as any man has ever suffered. Even though Job was righteous (Job 1:8, 21–22; 2:3, 10), he still passed through great pain—and he sought God to understand why. The Creator finally answered Job (chapters 38–41), overwhelming him with a sense of his power and majesty. As a result, Job exclaimed (42:2–4) that he now understood that God could do anything. In our case as well, sometimes our view of God is far too small, and God expands that view by sending afflictions and proving himself to be the all-powerful One on our behalf. Like Job, we draw closer to the Lord as we come to know him better.

Suffering also produces sanctification because it leads to intimacy with God. Again Job's case is instructive. Even though Job had grown in the Lord before his suffering, he needed to draw closer. At the end of his ordeal, his comments show that he had come to know God more deeply than he had ever known him before. He says, "My ears had heard of you but now my eyes have seen you" (Job 42:5). Job's mere hearsay knowledge of God became firsthand experience. There is nothing like affliction to change intellectual abstractions about God's sovereignty, comfort, and concern to concrete realities.

Affliction can stimulate sanctification in yet another way. God may use it to challenge the righteous to growth, instead of falling into sin. This point arises from James 1:1–12. There, the topic is clearly affliction, whereas later in James 1 the topic is temptation to sin. The typical Greek word for tribulation, affliction, or suffering is *thlipsis*. *Thlipsis* never appears in the New Testament in a context where it means temptation. On the other hand, the noun *peirasmos* and the verb *peirazo* are the usual words for temptation and to tempt. In several verses, they indicate a trial or testing (1 Pet. 4:12; Acts 9:26; 16:7; 24:6; Rev. 2:2, for examples). However, those verses don't emphasize affliction or suffering, but rather putting someone to a test.

In light of these basic New Testament uses of *thlipsis* and *peirasmos*, we would expect to find *thlipsis* in James 1:1–12 and *peirasmos* in verse 13 and following. Instead, *peirasmos* is used throughout the chapter, and *thlipsis* doesn't appear at all. This leads me to ask the following questions: Is James suggesting that afflictions are temptations or trials? Are all temptations afflictions? Are all afflictions temptations?

The answer to the first question is debatable, but the second and third questions are easier to answer. Are all temptations afflictions? Obviously, they are not. Some temptations come in the midst of afflictions (for example, the temptation to curse God that confronted the afflicted Job), but many times temptation arises without any accompanying affliction at all.

Are afflictions temptations? All afflictions are *potentially* temptations, because they provide an occasion for us to be tempted. For example, when one is angry at God, one is tempted to turn from him. We may yield to that temptation, but we may instead respond positively in faith and resist the temptation that came from our troubles. When we do resist, the affliction serves as a basis for growing closer to the Lord. Perhaps this is implicitly James's point in using *peirasmos* when the term *thlipsis* would seem to be the more natural choice of words.

A final way adversity promotes holiness is by offering sufferers the opportunity to imitate Christ. Many would love to imitate Christ if that meant having his power, glory, and authority over all things. We are called, however, to imitate Christ in other ways. Those who suffer for righteousness may suffer unjustly and for the sake of others. In so doing, they imitate the Savior's example (1 Pet. 3:17–18). Moreover, those who suffer as righteous may be required to bear that affliction and persecution without complaint. In so doing, they again follow the Lord's pattern (1 Pet. 2:23).

Jesus put in perspective the whole matter of what his disciples should expect. He said that "a student is not above his teacher, nor a servant above his master. It is enough for the student to be like his teacher, and the servant like his master" (Matt. 10:24–25). If the disciple is to be like his teacher, and if his teacher is Jesus, the disciple can expect to get from society the same thing Jesus did. The people of his own day nailed our Lord to a cross. Can Christian disciples realistically expect to escape persecution?

The apostle John confirms this point as well. He tells us that the children of God can expect their goals, values, and lifestyle to be misunderstood by those outside of Christ, and for the same reason that Christ was misunderstood (1 John 3:1). The world did not share or understand the Lord's goals and values. The result was that his enemies put him to death.

The more Christlike we become as children of God, the less we can expect to be understood and accepted by the world about us. And the more we can expect to incur the wrath of Satan and the world. Of course, as we imitate Christ in his sufferings, our sanctification or holiness is promoted.

The apostle Paul affirms this as well in Philippians 3. He relates that he left all of his former accomplishments and way of life to follow Christ. In verses 10–11 he states goals that any Christian should want:

> I want to know Christ and the power of his resur-
> rection and the fellowship of sharing in his suffer-
> ings, becoming like him in his death, and so,
> somehow, to attain to the resurrection from the
> dead.

Most Christians, if not all, would certainly desire the first two things Paul offers as his goals. We would love to know Christ better, and who wouldn't want to see in their own life the kind of power that raised Christ from the dead? As to the fellowship of Christ's sufferings, most of us would be happy to forgo that. However, Paul is right in listing this as one of his goals, because it is hard to comprehend how one could really get to know Christ and what he experienced without also undergoing afflictions for the sake of righteousness. We must remember as well that the power which raised Christ from the dead followed his unjust murder on the cross. At least in that case, the power wasn't divorced from the suffering. And so it often is with us. Only when we are totally overwhelmed by the trial and come to the end of our abilities to deal with it can we bring ourselves to leave it in God's hands and watch his awe-some power deliver us.

All of this means that even in the midst of the worst afflic-tion, God is at work to use suffering to draw us closer to him. That doesn't make the grief and pain any less evil, but it should encourage us to realize that affliction isn't a sign that God has abandoned us. Rather, he is using the pain and suf-fering to stimulate our growth in Christ.

CHAPTER 9

FROM PAINFUL TRIALS TO POSITIVE TESTIMONY

Some suffering moves beyond the general category of sanctification, because God uses it to prepare us for future ministry and blessing. For example, sometimes God permits affliction in the life of a godly person for the ministry that is possible in suffering. There are various ways afflicted believers can minister in spite of and even because of their distress. Those who experience adversity can have a tremendous testimony to those who don't know Christ as their personal Savior. Many non-Christians watch very closely how Christians react when they go through troubles. When they see the righteous experience affliction and remain faithful to the Lord, they are positively impressed. As Peter says (1 Pet. 3:15–16), their persevering faith and the positive testimony it gives not only puts to silence the negative thoughts of evil men, but also serves as a positive witness to those who don't know God personally through Christ.

Just as suffering provides a testimony to non-Christians, there is a ministry to Christians as well. Those who remain true to the Lord during hardship serve as an encouragement to others to remain faithful in spite of their own problems. Here Peter's words to suffering believers are appropriate. He encourages them to resist the devil and take a firm stand for Christ in spite of the afflictions they are enduring. Peter writes in relation to our adversary (1 Pet. 5:9):

Resist him, standing firm in the faith, because you know that your brothers throughout the world are undergoing the same kind of sufferings.

Peter's message is clear. You are not the only person suffering for Christ at the hands of Satan and his legions. All over the world there are brothers and sisters in Christ who are besieged with trials just as you are suffering. Take heart; you are not alone in this battle. Others are on the firing line, and they haven't surrendered to the enemy and turned from Christ. Don't you do that either! In addition, God uses suffering to prepare us to comfort others who undergo troubles (2 Cor. 1:3–4).

There is also a sense in which those who remain loyal to God in the middle of trials are actually ministering not only to others but to themselves. That is, as we cling to God in our suffering, he uses this to prepare us for even greater ministry. Here I think of the role affliction played even in the life of Christ to prepare him for further and greater ministry. In Hebrews 2:10 we read, "In bringing many sons to glory, it was fitting that God, for whom and through whom everything exists, should make the author of their salvation perfect through suffering."

The words "make perfect" don't refer to sinless perfection. That would make no sense in this case, for Christ has always been perfect! Instead, the words mean "to be brought to completeness or maturity." In other words, Jesus Christ in his humanity was prepared to be the complete Savior (everything a Savior should be) by means of enduring various afflictions, even before he went to the cross. If God could use adversity to prepare Christ to be our Savior, surely he can use suffering to prepare us for greater ministry.

God also uses pain and distress to prepare us for further trials. Just because one difficult trial hits us, that is no reason to think we have had our lifetime quota. Since we live in a fallen world, we can expect to face further affliction. In fact, there may be even greater and more severe trials yet to come. Had they come sooner, perhaps they would have destroyed us; but God in his goodness and grace prepares us for each new test. Part of that preparation involves confronting and enduring current pains and sorrows.

Think of Abraham. Suppose that in his *first* encounter with God he was required to offer up his son Isaac (Gen. 22). No doubt that would have been too much for him. God knew that, so he didn't give Abraham the most difficult trial until he had brought him safely through others. Faith and endurance, like other Christian virtues, can grow and develop. One of the ways God helps those virtues grow is by sustaining us successfully through our present trials. He knows exactly how much we can endure at any given moment. Part of God's program of giving us grace to endure each day is to prepare us to receive and use tomorrow's grace when we face that day's challenges.

Another general use of suffering in the lives of the righteous is to prepare them for judgment of their works. According to 1 Peter 1:7, affliction helps prepare the believer for the coming of Christ. After Christ returns for the church, all believers will give Christ an account of what they have done in their lives (2 Cor. 5:10 and 1 Cor. 3:10–15). In 1 Peter 1:7, Peter says that affliction helps prepare sufferers for that judgment so that their faith and actions will result in praise, glory, and honor when Jesus Christ is revealed.

The connection between suffering and reward may be unclear, but it can be explained. As we endure afflictions, we should become more Christlike, leading to lives that are likely to be filled with deeds that please God. At judgment time it will be evident that we have built lives of gold, silver, and precious stones, not ones of wood, hay, and stubble (1 Cor. 3:12–15). There will be rewards for lives pleasing to God. So, rather than interpreting hardship as a sign of God's displeasure, we should realize that God may be using it to prepare us for the day of judgment, when our endurance under fire serves as the basis of reward.

Moreover, God may use our afflictions as a basis for ultimately exalting us. Peter repeatedly teaches the theme of suffering and glory (1 Pet. 1:6–7, 11, 21; 2:12, 15, 19–21; 3:9, 14–22; 4:1, 4, 12–16, 19; 5:1–6, 9–10). The message is quite clear. Those who would be great in God's economy must first be brought low. Peter writes, "Humble yourselves, therefore, under God's mighty hand, that he may lift you up in due time" (1 Pet. 5:6). Affliction certainly helps to humble us, but regardless of how much we are humbled, suffering endured for righteousness' sake is clearly a prelude to exaltation. A beautiful example of this truth is Christ (1 Pet. 2:22; cf. Phil. 2:5–11). If we are finally to reign with Christ, we must follow his example of righteous suffering.

Finally, God may use our afflictions as a means to take us to be with himself. As life comes to an end, our final affliction will usher us into God's presence. This may not seem like a positive thing, but that may be because we don't fully agree with Philippians 1:21: "For to me, to live is Christ and to die is gain." Neither the apostle Paul nor I are suggesting that we should wish to die, or that death itself is good. The reason for death (sin) and the event itself are not good. But for the believer, death is the doorway to everlasting blessing in the presence of God. Therefore, the death of a Christian believer isn't necessarily a sign of God's displeasure. Affliction leading to death may well be God's way of promoting someone into his presence.

This completes my list of the uses of suffering. In a given instance, one or more of these may explain in part God's reasons for allowing evil to befall his people. Perhaps he is doing none of these things in a particular case. But when someone experiences affliction and is angry that God doesn't stop it, I believe that pointing to these uses of evil can help relieve the sufferer's feelings of confusion and anger. Of course, sometimes it is impossible to determine exactly why God allows suffering on a particular occasion. God may simply want to remind us that his ways are ultimately beyond our scrutiny. At some point we all need to let God be God, and know a few things we don't!

Sufferers may wrestle with a further question. The uses of suffering show that God is able to bring long-range good out of short-range evil. But isn't an all-powerful God also able to bring long-term good out of short-term good? If he can, why doesn't he? Scripture doesn't give us the answer, and I am not sure that we can know the answer for a certainty until we stand in the Lord's presence. I can, however, make a suggestion about what may in part be God's reason for not using short-range good to bring long-range good. My suggestion is this: God wants to work in our lives to accomplish his good purposes. In many cases, as we have seen, he wants to teach us something. But it is very hard to teach someone anything unless you have their attention. Affliction has a way of getting our attention like nothing else. Yes, God could bring long-range good out of short-term good, but when we experience nothing but blessing, we tend to be overly self-confident. We might not pay attention to God. If so, whatever else God wants to teach us through the experience will likely be lost.

Is this always the reason God brings long-term good out of short-term evil rather than out of short-term good? Only he knows for sure. But at least this suggests a possible reason for God's accomplishing his goals by means of suffering.

Often, we ask God to keep us from hardship and afflictions. When that doesn't happen, it is easy to become angry and to wonder why God doesn't respond. On the other hand, if we take seriously the fact that our world is fallen and that we are engaged in a spiritual war, we realize better why God doesn't always end our suffering. Rather than requesting exemption altogether from the battle and the wounds that come with it, Phillips Brooks's advice is wiser counsel:

Do not pray for easy lives; pray to be stronger people! Do not pray for tasks equal to your powers, pray for powers equal to your tasks. Then the doing of your work shall be no miracle, but you shall be a miracle. Every day you shall wonder at yourself, at the richness of life which has come to you by the grace of God.

CHAPTER 10

DECEIVED BY GOD?

*I*t has been more than a decade and a half since that fateful day when we first received the shocking diagnosis of Pat's condition. Though the stress and pain that first beset me have greatly subsided, they aren't completely gone. As Pat's condition gets worse, there are new frustrations and new sorrows as well as new battles to address in dealing with the symptoms of Huntington's Disease.

If Pat were gone, however, that wouldn't remove the pain. It would just add another reason for the tremendous hurt. Every now and again I hear of someone whose wife or husband died very suddenly. At times I have asked myself whether it would have been easier to lose Pat all at once or slowly, as is happening. Though I would want neither of these options, I have come to the conclusion that God is gracious in what he has allowed to happen in our case. I don't enjoy seeing what is happening to Pat, but even having my wife at two-thirds, one-half, or less of what she was is better than not having her at all. Still, whatever path God chooses for each of us, we know he will give the necessary grace to walk it.

In spite of all the lessons I have learned through these experiences, and in spite of all the sources of encouragement I have recounted, for many years I found especially troubling not just what was happening, but how it all had come about.

This is surely not a life I would have chosen. As I have shared, one of the most difficult things is that it appeared I did have a choice, for I didn't have to marry Pat. Once we married, we didn't have to have children. It seemed, however, that I made those choices under false pretenses. I was led to believe by God, or so it seemed, that I was choosing one sort of life, when in fact I wound up with exactly the life I was trying to avoid. In fact, I was saddled with a situation worse than anything I could have ever dreamed in my worst nightmare.

For a long time I was hurt and anguished by the thought that somehow God deceived me into marrying Pat by hiding information that could have saved me from my present circumstances. There were also questions about knowing and doing God's will. Was it really not God's will that I marry Pat and that we have children? Could I have been that mistaken about God's design for my life? Or was it really God's will that I marry her, but when one follows the Lord's leading one can expect to be double-crossed?

Such thoughts are among the most disturbing of all that have besieged me over the years, and they have been as disruptive to my relationship with the Lord as anything that I have ever experienced. I was raised in a home where a high premium was placed on telling the truth. If our word can't be trusted, what are we really worth? This is part of the very core of my outlook on and approach to life. How utterly distressing, then, when God, the very embodiment of truth, appeared to have deceived me!

In spite of all the other spiritual truths I have learned, I knew I would still feel uncomfortable with God until I sorted all this out. After many years of wrestling with these questions, and after most of my feelings of anger toward God were gone, I came to terms about whether or not I was deceived.

Was I deceived by God? I believe that I was in fact deceived, but not by God. Though it is hard to accept blame for such a critical error as this, I see now that I deceived myself. Given my background and the circumstances surrounding my meeting and marrying Pat, I constructed a case for a life relatively free of troubles. But that wasn't the only possible conclusion to infer from God's leading me to marry Pat and start a family. Let me explain.

My mother's illnesses and the strain they placed upon my father and his ministry made me conclude that anyone embarking on such a ministry would be best able to fulfill that work with a healthy wife and children. I knew that God was calling me to a life of scholarship, preaching, and teaching. I reasoned that whomever God would have me marry would be healthy or at least not so unhealthy as to jeopardize the ministry God was giving me. All of this seemed logical and reasonable enough.

I approached dating and marriage armed with such a mind-set, a very natural thing to do. Those raised in the home of an alcoholic, for example, would likely be very careful not to marry an alcoholic. I knew it would be possible to minister effectively if I had a wife whose health was poor, because I had seen my father do it. But it would be easier to minister without such a hindrance. God knew that, and so did I. I concluded, then, that if I was careful about such matters, God would probably not lead me to marry someone whose health would stand in the way of the work he had given me to do.

When Pat came into my life and we began to get serious about each other, we were very concerned about disobeying God's will. It was not the matter of her health that troubled us at that point, but rather the apparently incompatible forms of ministry to which we thought God was calling us. God

resolved that issue, however, in a way that neither of us origi-
nally expected, showing us that we could minister together
without contradicting his will for our lives in the slightest.
The only other question concerned Pat's health, but it was
exceptionally good at that time. There were no signs of what
was to come, and we were assured that what had happened to
her mother wouldn't be passed to Pat.

My love for Pat, my belief about the need to have a
healthy wife, my assurance that Pat wouldn't get her mother's
disease, and the clear leading of the Lord concerning our
respective ministries led me to conclude that God wanted us
together. Though such thinking is sound, it is still a clear
example of inferential reasoning.

Inferential reasoning is reasoning from things that are
clearly known to a conclusion that is not known but seems
necessitated by the things we do know. For example, Scripture
clearly teaches that there is only one God. Just as clearly, however, it refers to three distinct persons (Father, Son, and Holy
Spirit) as God. From such clear biblical truths, Christians
throughout church history have concluded that the right way
to think of God is as triune. Nowhere in Scripture do we find
the word *Trinity*, nor does any passage say that God is one as
to his essence or nature but three as to the manifestations of
that nature. Nonetheless, such a doctrinal conclusion seems
inevitable on the basis of what Scripture clearly teaches about
God.

Although the inference to the doctrine of the Trinity is a
natural and accurate inference, and although that doctrine is
certainly taught in Holy Scripture, inferential reasoning
is notoriously risky. From precisely the same information, it
may be possible to draw several conclusions. For example,
from the fossil records the atheistic scientist concludes that

evolution is correct; but from the same data, the Christian scientist finds scientific support and evidence for a Creator. How can this be since the "facts" are the same for both the Christian and non-Christian? This shows just how tricky inferential reasoning can be.

So it was in my case. From my reasoning about needing a healthy family in order to be free to minister, from the information we had at that time about Pat's health and the health of her family, from the Lord's leading regarding our respective ministries, and from the love he placed within us for each other, it was thoroughly logical to infer that we should marry and that health wouldn't curtail us. What I came to see some years ago is that while such inferences were natural ones to make and could have been correct, they weren't the only ones that were possible from the data we had. The conclusions I reached were reasonable, and they surely matched what I wanted to happen. But our best-case scenarios don't always match what God has planned for us, even when we think we can build a rational case that things are going to turn out just the way we want.

So where was the mistake in my thinking? Had God actually deceived me? Or had I mistakenly drawn the wrong inference from the information I had? I was certainly not wrong about my love for Pat, or hers for me. Nor was I mistaken that God wanted us to marry and minister together. I didn't have all the information I now know about Pat's health, but is God to be blamed for that? He could only be blamed for not giving me the pertinent information if he was *obligated* to give me that information before we married.

Yet what could possibly place God under such an obligation as that? For a long time I thought that the need for my wife to be healthy in order for me to accomplish my ministry was enough to obligate God to inform me somehow about the potential health risks of a prospective mate. That belief made me infer from the facts as I knew them at the time not only that I was to marry Pat, but also that she wouldn't have any major ongoing health concerns.

In believing all of these things, I deceived myself into thinking I was getting a different life than I have. Having called me to the ministry and having led me to Pat, God was only obligated to inform me of her family's medical history before we married if it would be impossible to carry on his work with a wife in poor health. In fact, it is not. From my dad's case, I knew that it was preferable for someone in ministry to have a healthy family. I also knew from his case that it is *possible* to minister very effectively even if your wife or other family members are in poor health. Moreover, I came to see that God's intended service for Pat and me is a bit different than we anticipated, and it is service we can do on behalf of the kingdom even though she has this serious illness!

The truth is that God had never promised me anything about my wife's health. I simply saw what I thought would be preferable for someone like myself, and I wrongly concluded that God would do it. It made logical sense, but it wasn't accurate.

Yes, I was deceived, but not by God. He didn't tell me anything that was false, nor did he mislead me. He wasn't obligated to inform me before we married that Pat was even at risk for Huntington's Disease, let alone that she would get it.

I have written much about being deceived by God. I have done so for several reasons. For one thing, it is such an important part of my own story. Beyond that, getting this question settled has been a major factor in fully restoring a positive attitude toward God. Sorting this issue out has solved a key intellectual problem, a problem that only heightened my own emotional and spiritual pain. What has happened and is still happening to Pat still hurts very deeply, but at least my frustration and anger over the situation are no longer directed toward God. Believe me, there is a very uneasy feeling that comes with being angry at the only person who can solve your problem. Thank God, that uneasy feeling and that anger are gone!

I have also shared this at length, hoping it will help my readers. Though no one's circumstances will be exactly identical to mine, we all need to be reminded how easy it is to build an incorrect case against God through inferential reasoning. Before looking at circumstances and inferring that God has deceived you or done anything else wrong, remember that the conclusion you are drawing may not be the only one possible. It is more likely that you are reading the evidence the wrong way. Before you accuse God over what you think he has done or failed to do, look again at the evidence, and be sure that you have interpreted it correctly. If you look long enough and hard enough, I am certain you will see that God isn't guilty of any wrongdoing, and that it is possible to read the evidence in such a way that it in no way implicates God in any deception or other evil.

What about the other question that began this book? Could one seek, find, and do God's will and get affliction in response? If by this we are asking whether God would respond to our obedience by sending affliction as a punishment, the answer is an obvious no. God doesn't send suffering as a punishment for doing his will. The Bible amply underscores that the one who obeys God will only receive blessing from God's hand in response to that obedience. The God of the Scriptures isn't an evil fiend who rewards us for obeying him by punishing us with pain and suffering.

On the other hand, there is more to the question than just this. While God won't *punish* with affliction for obeying his will, doing God's will doesn't guarantee that there will be no affliction when we obey. This sounds paradoxical, but it isn't. God won't send affliction in *punishment* for our obedience, but if we are faithful to God's plan, Satan won't be pleased. The adversary often takes out his displeasure by afflicting the people of God. The truth is that the more we are in the center of God's will, the more we are capturing ground against the enemy of God. Hence, the more we obey God's will, the more we can expect Satan's attacks on us in an effort to discourage and dissuade us from accomplishing God's purposes.

Yes, there will sometimes be affliction when we do God's will, but it doesn't come as punishment from God's hand. Scripture is very clear that those who follow God are engaged in a war with those who don't (Eph. 6:12; 1 Pet. 5:8–9). Satan will do his best to destroy us and our faith, but the Book of Job should encourage us to recognize that there is nothing he can do that the Almighty doesn't know, permit, and control. We are engaged in a spiritual war. Do we think we can go to war, even be in the front lines of the battle, and never be wounded?

I think many Christians naively think just that—if they think about spiritual warfare at all. I certainly never expected a wound quite like the one we got. I have come to see, however, that this expectation was unrealistic. The enemy is very real and has many ways of attacking those who would follow the Lord. Knowing there will be battle wounds doesn't mean the wounds don't hurt, but it can help us assess more accurately what has happened. One may wish exemption from the battle, but that isn't possible. One may even think of changing sides, as many do when confronted with tragedy, but that option isn't the answer to our problems for either time or eternity. And certainly it is far worse to arouse God's anger than to evoke Satan's!

In the years since this book was first published, many people who have heard or read about our situation have wondered about the next chapters of the story. They want to know how Pat and our sons are doing, and they also ask whether medical science has found a cure for this disease. In the next chapters I offer first an update and then further reflection on God's providence and purpose in our lives.

CHAPTER 11

BECAUSE PEOPLE ASK . . .

*I*t has now been many years since I first wrote any of the words that comprise this book. There have been many changes and challenges in my wife's condition, and all our sons are now in their twenties. Time moves on relentlessly and so does this disease, but the things I have shared in earlier chapters continue to be sources of encouragement and help. In addition, the Lord has blessed us in many different ways I couldn't have imagined in advance. From time to time some extra and unexpected blessing comes our way, and I always see this as God's way of telling us: "I just want you to know that I know what you're going through, I haven't forgotten about you, I'm still here for you, and this new blessing is my way of reminding you that I love you." I don't know whether many of these blessings would have come our way without us going through the trials of Pat's disease. Even if they otherwise would have happened, in our current context it all communicates God's love and care for us.

In this chapter I want to answer some of the most commonly asked questions people who know about Pat and my family raise. Perhaps as you've read the earlier chapters of this book, you have wondered about the things I'll discuss. First and foremost, people want to know how Pat is doing.

Sadly, I report that this disease is taking its toll. During the last five years especially, there have been some significant changes. We are now dealing with the advanced stages of this disease and are clearly closer to the end than the beginning. There have been numerous physical changes. It has become increasingly difficult for her to walk, and part of the reason is that she continues to have difficulty keeping her balance. She is not yet confined to a wheelchair, but we use one whenever she would otherwise have to walk a good distance. In addition, her speech has become slurred so that it is difficult to understand what she is saying much of the time. Conversations with her aren't impossible, but it takes a bit of effort by both parties for the talking to continue. I really miss the opportunity just to have a normal conversation with her.

In addition, Pat's motor skills have eroded, and her hand-eye coordination isn't very good. She increasingly needs help even with the basic essentials of getting dressed for each day. Because of these problems and others it became necessary in the fall of 2001 to begin feeding her through a tube surgically inserted into her stomach. I could add much more, but this gives you the basic picture.

Mentally, there has also been deterioration. Problems with memory are increasing, but the most noticeable change is that her attention span is quite limited. Her mind wanders, and that makes it hard for her to watch a movie or television program and follow what's happening. It is even harder for her to follow a sermon in church, and it is virtually impossible for her to read anything of much length. On some occasions she may stare at a printed page for half an hour and read it all, while on others she may just read one or two sentences repeatedly. If she's trying to read something longer, more often than not she eventually gives up trying to comprehend what she's reading, and puts the book or article down. These mental changes also make it difficult to have a conversation with her. You may ask a question and receive no answer for a minute or more. If you ask again, you find that the problem is one of several things: she didn't realize you were talking to her, she knew you were talking to her but couldn't focus adequately so as to offer a response, or she understood what you said, but it's just taking a bit of time for her to frame a response.

Because of both the physical and mental changes, it is no longer safe for me to be away from home even overnight. If I go anywhere for a day or more, I either take her with me or see that she stays with some friends who can handle her needs. This might seem to make it impossible for us to go anywhere, but so far that isn't so. In 2003 we took a number of trips out of town, out of state, and out of the country. Pat did well on these trips, and she loves to be with people and see and do different things. Traveling together is still enjoyable for us both. How long we will be able to continue making such trips is unclear, but she would rather get up and go than sit at home on the couch and watch television. The new experiences that come with travel are good for both of us.

As you can imagine, all of this means that there are increasing demands on my schedule to take care of her needs. However, new symptoms and needs develop slowly, so there is time to adjust. Tasks like giving her feedings through the feeding tube aren't nearly as difficult as I first thought they would be. Though her condition requires increasingly more of my time and work, it doesn't take long to work the new responsibilities into my schedule. What is truly difficult is the constant emotional drain of seeing my wife deteriorate before my eyes while I am helpless to do anything to stop that from happening. In fact, the "doing" of the extra chores Pat's condition requires, while work, is nothing in comparison to the emotional strain of what is happening.

In spite of what is happening to her, Pat continues to handle this extremely well. In all the years since she was diagnosed, she has never complained about having this disease or any of the specific symptoms that arise. She continues to view this as what God wants to do with her life, and she is willing to accept that. One of the many great things about her is that she refuses to give in to this disease. Whereas others would have given up long ago, Pat attempts to carry on with living as normally as possible. Depression is a major problem with Huntington's, but thankfully we have been able to address that problem with medication. As a result, she is happy with each new activity and opportunity for ministry, travel, or whatever.

When we do travel to minister, people who meet her are repeatedly overwhelmed by her. In particular, they see the way she handles her condition as a prime example of courage. I am so used to her satisfied disposition that when others mention her courage, it takes me a bit by surprise. But I have to agree with them. Though Pat knows what is happening to her (she is not out of touch with reality at this point), she isn't paralyzed by anxiety about the uncertainty of the future. Others faced with the prospects of this disease choose to commit suicide, but such a reaction isn't for Pat even an option.

One of the reasons I believe that Pat has adapted so well to what is happening stems from a basic aspect of her personality. She is not a complainer, and it is very easy to please her. In fact, she is the easiest person to please that I have ever known. It doesn't take much to make her happy, and she is appreciative of even the slightest thing done for her. In short, she is a very adaptable person because she isn't a demanding person. I think that is also why she handles what is happening to her so very well!

Next, people frequently ask how our children are doing. And they want to know if they have been tested for the disease or will be tested. All three sons are now in their twenties. Though they didn't talk much about what is happening as they grew up, there is no way that it didn't weigh on their minds and affect their plans for the future. For the longest time, if we asked any of them how they were doing with the possibility that they might get their mother's disease, they said they didn't really think about it. Whether that was really so, such responses made it difficult to talk with them about the disease and offer comfort, consolation, and encouragement.

As they have grown older, however, they have been more open about their thoughts and feelings. Our oldest son has said that his mom's having the disease and the possibility that he might get it have made a difference in everything. Our second son is clearly thinking about this, but has gone on to do doctoral work in English literature. When he made the decision to do so, I asked if he really wanted to commit to such a program of study in view of what might happen to him in relation to this disease. His response, I thought, was most appropriate, though it isn't always easy for people at risk for Huntington's to see things this way. He said that even if he gets this disease, it will take awhile for it to develop. In the meantime, he has to do something with his life, and of course, it's always possible that he won't get it. Whether or not he gets the disease, he must do something with his life, and his interest in English literature is the most logical thing to pursue. I concur with his decision, in part because none of us has any guarantee about the length or quality of our life. Any of us could die at a relatively young age; does that mean we shouldn't pursue or have pursued the careers and interests we did because we might die young? Of course not! All of us have a limited number of years on this earth; it behooves us to get on with accomplishing whatever we are going to do in life, and to do so sooner, not later!

Our youngest son has had a difficult time in deciding what he wants to do in life. I am confident that the possibility of getting Huntington's affects that greatly. This is especially so, because he has said on several occasions that he is certain that he will get the disease. When asked how he could know that, he answers that he just knows. When reminded that it is just as likely that he won't get it as that he will, that doesn't seem to be much comfort. This belief that he will certainly get the disease isn't the most rational, but it is very real and understandable. If you prepare yourself for the worst, then if it happens, you can always say you thought it would. If it doesn't happen, then there will be a pleasant surprise. In either case, expecting the worst seems to be a safe strategy. However, even if you anticipate the worst and it is confirmed, there is no way that expecting the disease can properly prepare you to get it. No matter how much you try to prepare yourself for the worst, the fact is still that you have an equal chance of not getting it as your chance of getting it. When the disease is actually confirmed (by test or by expression of the symptoms), that shatters all hope of escaping the disease, and it is dubious that anything can quite prepare one emotionally and mentally for such a diagnosis.

As to being tested for Huntington's, none of our sons has done that yet. I think many people believe this simply involves taking a blood test, but that is not so. There is the test, but it is preceded by a series of counseling sessions, and there is more counseling once the test is taken and results are divulged. Even if one learns that he won't get the disease, there is still a certain emotional fallout. Though the odds that other siblings will get the disease remain the same, it is not unusual for the sibling whose test shows that he won't get the disease to think that because he has escaped, it is more likely that one or more of his siblings will get the disease. Thoughts of this sort invariably cause the one who has escaped to feel guilty for escaping while other family members probably won't.

In addition to these aspects of the testing process, there are other implications. As mentioned in earlier chapters, those who are known to have the gene may find it impossible to get a job or secure health insurance. Then, there is also the likelihood that if unmarried at the time one learns of the disease, it may be impossible to find someone who will marry you. Even if you don't know that you have the gene but only that you are at risk, this may well scare away any prospective mate. With all of these dimensions to the testing process, some people would prefer not to be tested and not to know this information. However, without it, it is rather difficult to make major life decisions about career, marriage, and (if married) children.

So, the decision to take the test is not an easy one. I have wrestled with whether or not to have our sons tested. Before the exact genetic marker was known, there seemed to be good reason not to test them, especially since they were rather young at the time. As they grew older and the gene for Huntington's was identified, getting tested made more sense, but even so it is a hard decision. Some years ago, however, I came to a conclusion about my own response to this issue. I concluded that what is at stake are my sons' lives. Since it is their lives, they should have the right to decide whether they take the test. And my response should be to support them and whatever decision they make. My personal preferences need to be set aside. My oldest son has decided that he would prefer not to know this information, so he would only get tested if he were contemplating marriage or some other major decision. Our second son has said that he wants to be tested, but so far nothing has been done. For a number of years he has lived away from home, so it would have been difficult for us to provide the personal support we would want to give any of our sons going through this process. And it isn't just any doctor, clinic, or hospital that does this test, so all of that complicates the process. Our youngest son hasn't said whether he wants to be tested; it may be that he hasn't yet decided what to do, and that is surely understandable.

Another question people frequently ask has to do with research on the disease and whether a cure is on the horizon. Though geneticists and physicians continue to learn more about this disease, unfortunately a cure still eludes them. Researchers have identified the genetic configuration in Huntington's patients. The gene involved, dubbed *huntingtin*, is actually present in all human beings. It is just that in patients with this disease there is mutant huntingtin; this expresses itself by a large number of repetitions of the genetic sequence involved. Scientists have been able to produce Huntington's-like symptoms in laboratory mice. Still, the major questions before researchers are exactly what mutant huntingtin does to kill cells, and why it only kills cells in one part of the brain, even though it is present in other parts of the brain.

A December 2002 article in *Scientific American*, authored by a professor at a university in Milan, Italy, and her two postdoctoral lab assistants, explained the challenges facing Huntington's researchers. As she and her colleagues show, there are several different theories on how mutant huntingtin kills brain cells. Each theory leads to a different program of research, and it may turn out that answers to various questions the researchers are pursuing may in fact be the "flip" side of other questions and their answers. Clearly, researchers have a long way to go, but at least they have some theories and a strategy for addressing this disease. How long it will take to pursue each lead is hard to predict, but it is encouraging that research goes on.

Despite grounds for encouragement, research on this disease has raised distinct ethical questions. Most specifically, one strategy of addressing the disease is to replace some of the cells lost. In cases where this has been done, patients have regained some mental and/or physical functions they had lost. Still, ethical questions arise because the best "candidate" for such a procedure is tissue from aborted fetuses. A second possible option is material from stem cells, but that also raises ethical questions.

These developments aren't entirely unforeseen by some of us. For a long time, I have thought that gene-splicing technology might eventually be the way to change the aberrant genetic sequencing to a normal sequence. However, at most that would stop further loss of brain cells, but it wouldn't replace cells already lost. And therein lies the ethical dilemma of where to get replacement brain cells, because it is likely that fetal tissue would be used for this process. None of this means that research should stop, but only that the challenges ahead won't only be scientific and genetic, but ethical as well.

Then, invariably people want to know how I am doing with what is happening to my wife. I share with them various things from the material in this book. I am still convinced that God's grace doesn't require him to exempt us from this trial in the first place or to stop it now. I am also convinced that God didn't mislead me about his will for my life. Over the years I have been led to reflect more on God's providential control and his specific purposes for my life and that of my wife. In the next chapter, I want to share those thoughts with you.

CHAPTER 12

PROVIDENCE
AND THE PURPOSE
OF OUR LIVES

In thinking about things that have happened in my life, some might say there is little evidence of God's control or concern. Rather, my life has been driven one way or another by random events that have no relation to one another. Hence, there is little evidence that even if God cares about the details of our lives, his hand has been upon my life. On the contrary, however, as I think back over my life, I can see God's hand in it to move me to do certain things he intended me to do.

It is clear to me that one of the major things God wanted to do with my life was to prepare me to deal with tragedy so that I would ultimately think even more deeply about the problem of evil, write about it extensively, and preach and teach on this topic. In addition, all along God knew that Pat would get this disease, and he wanted her to have someone to care for her, and he chose me to be the one. Let me address each of these purposes independently, though to a certain extent they are interrelated.

Many things in my background have already prepared me to work and minister in relation to the problem of evil. I have already shared about the concerns raised by my mother's health. These experiences stimulated in me an interest in the problem of evil. Because of that interest, my education at several schools made that issue a focus of my thinking and work for the various degree programs in which I enrolled.

All of that work and thought, however, might have stayed with me alone if not for God's call to ministry. Relatively early in my life, I sensed the Lord wanted me in full-time ministry. By the time I entered high school, I was convinced the Lord wanted me to train others for ministry—a teaching ministry similar to my dad's seemed the clear direction God had in store for me. As I grew up, however, I never envisioned the specific subject matter I would pursue in school and as a teacher and writer. It was only after I was in seminary taking course work for the foundational ministry degree that I realized my greatest interest was theology. It wasn't until I initially entered doctoral work that I realized how much philosophy interested me and how important it is to systematic theology. By the time I reached my doctoral dissertation, I knew I wanted to work on the problem of evil, but I doubted that I could do this at a major secular university. I still marvel at the open-mindedness of my professors and the university in allowing me not only to work on this issue but also to defend a theistic position.

Given my background and upbringing, it is easy to see why I would have such an interest in the problem of evil. You can also see how my earlier degree theses on the Book of Job and on God's sovereignty in relation to human freedom both stimulated and prepared me to work on the problem of evil for my dissertation. I completed my doctoral program in 1978, but I began teaching in 1976. The issue of God and evil arose in a number of courses I taught. I could see how so much in my life had led me to the teaching ministry I was having. After my graduation in 1978, I just assumed that I would continue teaching and writing on this topic (together with others). I thought I had worked out good answers to this issue. Of course, if I was to communicate the content of my studies to everyday people, I knew that I would have to revise my material to make the same points without all the technicalities one would expect in a doctoral dissertation. But I believed I had the basic answers to this problem. That was nine years before we received Pat's diagnosis.

When the diagnosis of Pat's disease came, I was totally shocked and surprised. I have already shared how all my previous academic work was of no comfort at that time. I see God's hand, however, in the ordering of these events in my life. If we had received the diagnosis before I had done the intellectual work, I probably would have spent a lot of time searching for solutions in philosophical discussions of the topic. By leading me through the academic journey before having to deal with real suffering in a personal way, God in effect was preparing me to look elsewhere than my academic study for answers to what was happening in my life and why. Without such a "narrowing" of my options, I might have searched fruitlessly for years for answers to the questions and needs Pat's disease has raised. So I can see clearly the Lord's hand in the very timing of these events in my life.

I can also see God's hand in what I have done with all my thinking about the religious problem of evil. Shortly after receiving my Ph.D. from the University of Chicago I was able to get my dissertation published, but it didn't stay in print very long. I approached another publisher and received a contract to revise the book somewhat and reprint it. I believe this contract came before we found out about Pat's condition. Once we did learn about it, everything seemed to be put on hold in my life, including my work on publications. When I eventually returned to my work on the problem of evil, I found that the academic discussion had changed significantly in the intervening years since I finished my dissertation. Hence, many new chapters were written for the reprinted version. As I worked on those chapters, I began to think that maybe the best way to make my point that the religious problem of evil is a different kind of problem from the others would be to write about my wife and family. I concluded that if I did this, I would have to adopt a much more direct, nontechnical style, and I had to share explicitly my thoughts and feelings about what was happening; otherwise, the material probably wouldn't help anyone, especially suffering people, very much.

Somewhat reluctantly, I wrote two relatively brief chapters that were included in my longer work on the academic problem of evil. The manuscript was delivered to the publisher in 1993, and I thought that would be the end of what I would do on this topic. But God had other plans. When editors at the press read those two chapters on the religious problem of evil, they immediately encouraged me to take that material out of the original book, expand it, and publish it as a more popular level book. I appreciated their endorsement of the work, but I was hesitant to do what they suggested. However, as I thought further about their suggestion and began to speak to classes about Pat's condition and what the Lord was teaching me through it, I received many positive reactions to this material. In addition, people who read the longer work often commented on the helpfulness of the two chapters on the religious problem. After further thought and prayer, I concluded that even though I wasn't eager to write this other book, if the Lord wanted to use it to help other people, I shouldn't stand in his way. The result eventually was a popular-level volume on the religious problem, a work that comprises much of the content of this current book.

It is quite clear to me, then, that one of the things God wanted to do with my life was to bring me through the experiences I've had with evil and suffering so that I would write, teach, and preach on these themes, with the ultimate intention that what I would say and do would help hurting people deal with tragedy and would also help those who minister to the afflicted. Though I thought God wanted me to write and teach about the problem of evil before we received Pat's diagnosis, I thought the content of what I would say was one thing. Without dealing with Pat's disease and its implications, I could not have written this more popular-level book. Moreover, I certainly couldn't present from the pulpit the more technical academic ideas from my dissertation; but when I speak about our struggles with suffering, there are many who come to hear and respond positively to what they hear.

Clearly, God's hand has been involved in all of this. I also see his hand in another factor that has contributed to my work on the various problems of evil. In an earlier chapter, I wrote about God's hiding the future from us so that I wouldn't hesitate over health issues to marry Pat. There is another respect in which God has hidden the future from all of us, and I think it has contributed to the work I've done on the religious problem. As mentioned in previous chapters, there is currently no known cure for Huntington's Disease. I believe that there is a cure for this disease and that God knows what it is, but so far he hasn't divulged it to anyone who has the disease or is at risk, nor has he revealed it to researchers working on this disease. I don't know and can't predict when that information will be revealed; everyone who knows about this disease hopes it will be sooner rather than later.

Suppose that a cure had been available even before Pat was diagnosed, or that it had been revealed shortly after we learned the dreadful news. The disease would still be a horrible disease, but there would be far less emotional turmoil over what is happening if a cure were known. I think it is safe to say that without the stress of dealing with an incurable, terminal disease, I would not have questioned so thoroughly why and how this could be happening, and I wouldn't have discovered many of the things I have shared in this book.

Please do not misunderstand this. I am not suggesting that God has withheld information about a cure for this disease just so that I would have time to think through these issues and write this book. Nor am I saying that a delay in finding a cure has made it good that Pat got this because of what I've learned as we await the discovery of a cure. I don't know why God hasn't allowed researchers to discover a cure yet. But I do know that the delay has been instrumental in accomplishing God's intentions for my specific life-history during the years since 1987, when we learned about this disease. My own thought and work about the various problems of evil has been spurred in part by the fact that no cure is currently known, that is, God has used this in my life to accomplish some of the things he wanted to do in and through me.

I also believe that God had another major intention for me, and it relates to marrying Pat. God's intent was to provide someone to manage Pat's needs and take care of her, and I am that someone. Whether Pat and I had ever met, let alone married, and whether she had married anyone, let alone me, God knew she would get this disease and would need someone to take care of her, especially as she would become less able to care for herself. That she would get this disease was determined the moment she was conceived.

Over the last decade or so as I have helplessly watched Pat's condition worsen, it has occurred to me on many occasions that the point of this marriage is not about me, but about her. Pat's father is in his eighties and in need of significant care himself. It is unclear that any other immediate or extended family member would take the role of Pat's caregiver. God knew she would need someone, and he provided me.

What I am suggesting may sound contrary to much Christian thinking about the purpose of marriage. Early in life Christians are taught that marriage is God's idea, and that his intent was to provide a helpmate for man. God said that it is not good for man to be alone. To satisfy the need for a companion and partner, God created woman. It is natural, then, for men to marry in order to find a wife who will help them with their life's work. In my case, I knew I needed a wife to help with my ministry. When I met Pat, I had no problems with her having a call to full-time ministry, for I believed she could and would basically fulfill that call as my wife. That wouldn't mean she couldn't also minister apart from my ministry, but helping me would be a major part of her life. So I adopted the common Christian understanding of marriage.

I want to affirm as strongly as possible that Pat has, indeed, been a wonderful wife and supporter and helper of my ministry. But in light of her condition, I have to believe that God's purpose in bringing us together is as much (if not more so) to provide someone to care for her as it is to give me a helper for my ministry. And I want to say as plainly and clearly as I can that if this is the major purpose of my marrying Pat, I have no problem with that. It is a privilege to be her husband, and I am more than willing to do whatever is needed to care for her. If the tables were turned, I have no doubt that she would eagerly care for me.

Some may read this and respond that while this has happened to us, we can hardly say that God's intention (even his main intention) with our marriage is to provide someone to care for Pat. It's just something that has turned out that way, but God's providence did not do this. I disagree, and I want to explain further why I disagree.

Looked at from one perspective, I suppose it might appear that all of this has happened somewhat by chance. Indeed, when you think about it, you have to think it was a long shot that Pat and I would ever even meet, let alone marry and raise a family. Pat was raised in upstate New York in North Syracuse. Wheaton, Illinois, was the farthest west Pat had ever been, and that hadn't happened until she entered an M.A. program at Wheaton College in 1971.

As for me, I'm three years older than Pat. I was born in Dallas, Texas, but raised in Southern California from the time I was two years old. I had heard of Syracuse, New York, but the basic thing I knew about it was that Syracuse University, located in that town, had a pretty good football team. I had been to Chicago a few times to visit my brother who went there in 1966 to take a teaching position at Moody Bible Institute, but most of my life had been lived in Southern California. When I did move to the Chicago area in 1971, it was to attend Trinity Evangelical Divinity School, not Wheaton College. It wasn't until late February, 1972, that I met Pat, and even then, that happened on a blind date.

With such diverse backgrounds, what are the chances that Pat and I would ever meet? But that underscores my point: none of this has happened by chance. If we were to calculate the odds of what has happened, they would be astronomically stacked against any of this ever occurring. And yet it did. One can choose to say that all of this is purely a happy series of coincidences coming together by chance. However, with everything I have shared about our story, I trust that you can see why it makes much more sense to see God's providential hand involved in our lives to bring these things to pass. It is in large part because I believe so strongly that God's hand has brought these things to pass that I am willing to accept the various roles God intended me to fulfill.

Some people, hearing our story and seeing us together after all that has happened, offer me encouraging comments about the fact that Pat and I are still together and that I am handling her needs. They respond as though what I am doing is unusual and praiseworthy. I appreciate those sentiments, but the truth is that I'm just an ordinary guy who is deeply in love with his wife. And there isn't any diagnosis of any disease that could ever change that! I don't know the exact course Pat's disease will take, but I know that whatever it is, I have to be there. As unsettling as this disease and its progression are, I couldn't relax even slightly if I didn't know that Pat's needs were being cared for properly.

Beyond all of this, there is the matter of our wedding vows. Either one means what one promises when one promises to stay together and love each other in *sickness* and in health, or those vows should be dispensed with. If we can't keep this set of most significant and most personal promises, why should anyone ever believe any other promise we make? But the main thing that drives me to be with Pat, regardless of what happens, is my love for her.

Having said these things about divine providence, there is one further point I must make about God's will. I believe it is important in seeking God's will to distinguish between God's will and his way, and there is also God's timing. My point is that at times we feel led by the Lord to do something, but we also mentally construct the way it will happen and the timing. In contrast, God plans it in a different way and with different timing. When events start to play out and things don't go exactly as we thought, it is very natural to question whether we have misread God's will altogether. In the aftermath of receiving Pat's diagnosis in November 1987, I know that I raised just that question. I had figured out what I thought God wanted me to do, and I had constructed my plan for how it would happen. When I learned that things weren't going to happen the way I had thought, the natural reaction was to wonder whether the path taken really was God's will.

In fact, I believe that God wanted Pat and me to marry, that he had called both of us to full-time ministry, and that he wanted us to have the children we have. I just expected all of this to happen in a different way than it did, a way that I had constructed as a best-case scenario. What I needed to do was readjust my thinking to the reality that even if we know what God wants us to do (his will), that doesn't automatically dictate the way his will comes to pass. And it certainly doesn't mean that we can do whatever we want in whatever way and timing we choose, so long as the result is what we sensed as God's will for us. God's will must be done in his way and in his time. Readjusting my thinking to God's way was painful but necessary. But as I have shared in this chapter, I can now see that the way events have happened is the way God intended to accomplish his will in Pat's life and my life. Could he have done this in some other way? Only he knows the answer to that. But he certainly knew that the way things have happened was a way to move us to do his will. Believing that God is all-wise, I also must believe that the way he chose was the proper way to bring about his will in our lives.

And the results? The Lord did want me to marry Pat and to have a ministry of teaching, preaching, and writing; it's just that all of this has happened under different circumstances from those we had envisioned and with a slightly different emphasis than I had in mind. In addition, God wanted both Pat and me to serve him on the mission field. Since 1985, we have traveled together and ministered on many occasions literally all over the world. We had thought of missions in terms of long-term missions, but God's way has been for us to go as short-term missionaries during summer vacation time to teach those training for ministry and to preach in a variety of settings. In fact, in summer 2001 we even made it to Africa, ministering both in South Africa and Zimbabwe.

There is God's will and there is God's way, and all of this must be within his timing. I have learned the need to think "outside the box" of our notions about how God will accomplish his will in our lives. It is, of course, possible that anyone may have misjudged both God's way and his will, but we need to be open to the possibility that while we are reading God's goal for us correctly, we must be flexible enough to let him accomplish it in his own way.

As I conclude this chapter and book, I hope that this book has ministered to you, and that it will help you serve others who are hurting. This has not been an easy book to write, and I would give anything not to have learned what I have through these experiences. But if this book helps you, it will have been worth the effort to write it.

As for me and my family, the story continues. Just as there have been surprises already (some welcome, some unwelcome), God probably has others in store. Do I have any regrets over marrying Pat and having a family? In many respects, that is an impossible question to answer. If it means would I have married her if I knew then what I know now, that doesn't make the question any easier. If I knew then what I know now, I would have known what a blessing from God she and my sons would be. I would have known all the problems I'd avoid by not marrying her, but I'd also have known of the lost blessings. Would I give back those incredible blessings to escape the trials we have experienced? Who would be so foolish, even if they thought they could guarantee an easier set of trials or avoid troubles altogether?

I do know some things for a certainty, though. I know that throughout eternity I'll be thanking God for the wife and family he gave me and for the ministry he has allowed us to have in spite of (and even because of) the many hardships. I also know that when the wounds from the spiritual warfare in which we all are engaged come—and they will come—we will need the comfort and care of God. In spite of our reactions, even if we suspect or actually accuse him of wrongdoing, I am so thankful that he is patient with us and is always ready to give his comfort and care!

AFTERWORD

by Patricia S. Feinberg

I would like to tell you what God has done in my life. As my brother and I were growing up, our mother suffered with a mysterious disease. I did not know the name of the disease, nor the specifics of it, because we were not told. My personal opinion was that it was a mental illness, and most of my mother's symptoms suggested that to me. It was only much later that we would learn she had Huntington's Disease.

My family was not a Christian family at the outset, but the Lord gave both my mother and me a desire to know him. My mother sold Avon products for a while, and she made a friend on her route who was a Christian. My mother's friend invited her to an evangelistic meeting where she accepted Christ. The pastor from the friend's church came over and talked with my father, who also became a Christian. My brother and I came to the Lord when a missionary candidate from the church came to talk with us.

I was nine years old at the time. As God gave me a desire to follow him, I started reading my Bible every day and attending the church. Over the years I became very involved in the church.

The youth pastor in the church had been a missionary to Africa, and he was a great influence on me. When he preached at a missionary conference where an invitation was given for young people to follow the Lord completely in their lives, I turned my life over to God for whatever he wanted me to do. I thought he might want me on the mission field, so I took steps to prepare myself for that. I went to Nyack College, in part because it had a strong reputation for training missionaries. After graduation, I applied to some mission boards, but nothing opened up. I went on to Wheaton College for an M.A. degree in Christian education. I felt such additional training would help me in mission work, and I thought that after further academic work, the Lord would open up the opportunity for me to go to the mission field.

While at Wheaton, our prayer group prayed that if the Lord had a husband for us, he would bring him along at the right time. One of my friends in the group was dating a student at Trinity Evangelical Divinity School, and she arranged a blind date for me with another seminarian attending Trinity.

As it turned out, John and I dated not just once but many times. As our relationship grew, the Lord made it clear the he wanted us to marry. We felt certain that God had led us together. After several years of marriage, we were blessed with three special boys who have been a continual joy to us.

In the midst of raising a family and sharing in John's ministry, I learned in the fall of 1987 that I have a genetic neurological disease called Huntington's Chorea. It involves premature deterioration of the brain, and it has severe mental and physical effects. In addition, it shortens one's life. Though I was shocked when this disease was diagnosed, I knew that when physical problems come, one should thank God for his presence and strength in the midst of those problems, rather than becoming bitter. And I knew that I should do that whether I felt like it or not; so that's what I did on the way home in the car. I also knew 1 Thessalonians 5:18, which says, "Give thanks in all circumstances, for this is God's will for you in Christ Jesus." No matter what the circumstances, God is still there, and he is in control of all that happens. He is faithful to his Word. That is reason for thanksgiving, and I continue to thank him each day.

The next months were very difficult for both John and me, going through the process of accepting what had happened. One thing that was very helpful to me was that as I read through the Book of Psalms, I wrote down every reference having to do with God's strength in time of trouble. The main one was Psalm 46:1: "God is our refuge and strength, an ever-present help in trouble." God made that verse true in my life. I have confidence in his presence, even in the midst of this disease.

I have been trying to figure out what God wants me to learn from this, and what he wants me to do about it. One thing the Lord has reinforced to me is that I am just clay in his hands. As Paul says in Romans 9:20, "But who are you, O man, to talk back to God? 'Shall what is formed say to him who formed it, "Why did you make me like this?"'" God has the right to do anything he wants with me. Who am I to complain?

I gave myself to Christ as a teenager for whatever he wanted—without reservation. Though what has happened is not at all what I imagined, I cannot complain. I said he could do with me as he chose. Far from complaining, my responsibility is to thank God for doing his will in my life.

Another thing God has done through this illness is to make me face life and death issues and to see the absolute necessity of making the most of the time I have left. It is easy for all of us to think there will be enough time to do what needs to be done for the Lord. We tend to plan to serve him, but always later. My experience is a vivid reminder that no one of us has a guarantee of how long our life on earth will be or what kind of life we will have. Whatever God calls us to do in service of the kingdom needs to be done sooner, not later.

Another Scripture that God has used in my life is 2 Corinthians 1:3–4: "Praise be to the God and Father of our Lord Jesus Christ, the Father of compassion and the God of all comfort, who comforts us in all our troubles, so that we can comfort those in any trouble with the comfort we our-selves have received from God." The Lord has given me such complete comfort that I want to find ways to share it with others.

My disease has also offered witnessing opportunities. One opportunity that John and I had was the chance to witness to my Jewish neurologist. John went with me to see her, and she came right out and asked us what he was doing teaching in a Christian seminary when he has a Jewish last name. In telling her how his family came out of Judaism to Christ, he was able to share the gospel with her. The other thing that she could not understand was how calm we were about the whole thing.

I consider it another blessing of the Lord that the disease for many years progressed very slowly. That has amazed the doctors from the beginning, and it gives us a further opportu-nity to witness to them. When they express their amazement, we make a point to share our belief that my disease and my very life are in God's hands. I believe the course the disease has taken is a result of God's intervention on my behalf.

It has been many years since we learned that I have Huntington's. God has been so faithful to me, and I thank him for his faithfulness, love, and comfort. It is my hope that what I have shared will be a comfort and encouragement to you, the readers. I want to say to those who are suffering that God is sufficient!

NOTES

Chapter 1

1. Alvin Plantinga, *God, Freedom, and Evil* (Grand Rapids: Eerdmans, 1974), 63–64.

Chapter 7

1. John S. Feinberg, *The Many Faces of Evil*, expanded and reprinted ed. (Wheaton, IL: Crossway, 2004).

2. The questions of why the unrighteous suffer and how God uses affliction in their lives are also important. However, the more troublesome religious problems focus on righteous suffering. While God may use affliction in the life of unbelievers to accomplish some of the same goals he intends for believers, he might also use affliction of the unbelieving as punishment for their sin. It should also be clear that in speaking of righteous sufferers, I am not referring to people who are sinlessly perfect. Only Christ fits that category. Rather, I refer to those believers whose basic pattern of life is to follow God and avoid evil.